SOBRIETY

DELIVERED

Everything

ALCOHOL

PROMISED

JUSTINE WHITCHURCH

This book deals with alcohol abuse and mental illness. If you or a person you know is in need of crisis support, please call the following numbers:

Lifeline on 13 11 44

Kids Helpline on 1800 55 1800

SANE helpline on 1800 187 263

ADF (Alcohol and Drug Foundation) 1300 858 584

Alcoholics Anonymous 1300 222 222

Beyond Blue 1300 224 636

You can also visit eheadspace.org.au or https://www.lifeline.org.au/get-help/online.

Call 000 if there is an emergency.

TABLE OF CONTENTS

PROLOGUE

THE VIBRANT WOMAN I am today is in stark contrast to the woman I was 15 years ago—a lost and much defeated alcoholic mum of two who was knocking on death's door.

In 2012, at the age of 39, I almost lost my life to alcohol addiction. It was the grand finale to years of self-medicating to cope with anxiety, depression, a highly toxic first marriage, subsequent divorce, great financial loss, the diagnosis of my daughter with type 1 diabetes and, to a lesser degree, life's everyday challenges.

Healthwise, my liver was failing, my platelet count was dangerously low, and I had excessively high triglyceride levels. Not to mention side effects like hair loss, no menstrual cycle for nine months, unexplained broken bones, and daily bouts of diarrhoea.

All of these physical symptoms were unforgivingly being carried by a 47kg skeletal body.

One day, my daughter, Evie, looked at me with tears in her eyes and said, "Mum, I am scared you are not going to get better."

Her fear was as real as my pain. My life was hanging on by a thread.

But I survived. I recovered. In fact, I thrived.

And this is how I did it.

PREFACE

WHEN I WAS A GIRL

BEFORE I BEGIN to tell you how I rose from what I can only describe as the "depths of hell", I should tell you about the series of events that threw my mental health so far off-kilter and provide an overview of my life before addiction to alcohol.

The reason I give you my backstory is not to lie blame on any one single person or event or suggest that this is the reason I drank.

At the end of the day, I am the one who picked up the drink and didn't put it back down.

I take full responsibility for what I did to myself and others.

I was born on the 19th April 1973 to Lesley and Donat Santowiak in the Victorian South-Eastern Gippsland town of Traralgon.

My mum had immigrated from England only a few years prior, following the path of her own parents and three younger brothers, and my dad and his family immigrated from Poland in 1964 at the age of 14. Both were still adjusting to the differences between living in large European cities and now a very small country town. My mum worked various secretarial jobs once arriving, whilst my dad had forged his path into a mechanical drafting role at the local SEC power station after arriving in the country speaking no English at all. At the young ages of 20 and 21, they were married, and before they could blink, I came along. With both of them working, I spent a great deal of time with my nana on my mum's side and this resulted in an extraordinarily strong bond. My nan really did become my second mum and I relied on her in many ways.

She was my rock.

At the age of six, my parents separated. My memories of this time are vague, yet distinct. I remember my mum packing up our belongings and telling me we were going to live with my nana and grandad, and at the time, it didn't seem like such a bad thing because it was familiar. My dad was helping us with the process. To be honest, I can't remember an angry or hostile environment or any harsh words being spoken during this time, or for that matter, much before the separation. Whether that is an accurate recall or simply two parents that were extremely good at keeping this behind closed doors, I am not sure. But that part of the separation didn't affect me.

My mum and I moved into the spare room at my nan's and I distinctly remember that even though there were two single beds, I always wanted to sleep with my mum. There was definitely some fragility in my emotions starting to come to the surface and I was beginning to see a lot of 'fear' in some very normal things.

My nana was a 'checker' and a desperate worrier. Whenever we left the house, she would pull the power cords out from the wall, check the oven that had not been used since the night before, and ensure the windows and doors were locked several times amongst a myriad of other things. As a little girl, I watched this and took it into my subconscious.

In saying that, my dad also had a 'thing' for cleanliness and order, something he too had inherited from his mum. Our home was meticulous, everything was labelled and in order, meals were eaten at the table with a tea towel on our lap, and the constant cleaning of surfaces was hard to keep up with.

In fact, there is a story that I was told later in life that demonstrates just how this may have infiltrated my own way of thinking. At the age of three, my mum had been diligently toilet training me, and for those of us that have undertaken this with our own children, we all know the most important part is the child 'telling' us they need to go in the first place. After a day out, we were coming down the driveway and walking towards the back porch. I then politely advised my parents that I needed to go to the toilet, but probably a little too late. My mum was over the moon as I had actually given some notice, but for my dad, there was a panic and a rush to get the back-door open so I didn't wee on the concreted landing. As it turns out, I didn't make it and I wet my pants and leaked a pool of urine onto the porch.

My dad muttered something to 'himself' and then rushed off to get his bucket of disinfectant, the scrubbing brush, and the hose whilst my mum picked up a sobbing little me inside to clean up. Whilst this story horrifies my dad today, this was just a symptom of someone whose internal standards of perfectionism prioritized the way they functioned. Nothing more and nothing less.

Dad in his early days as a Mechanical Draftsman in the late 70's.

Mum in 1972 after immigrating to Australia.

Me as a newborn with Mum, Dad, Grandad & uncle
Mike.

I loved being in front of the camera from as early as I can
remember.

Even brought my props for the photos!

Happy was I in front of the lens.

Say 'cheese'. (aged 3)

My muchly loved Grandad, Nana (my 2nd Mum) and I.

Dad, Mum and I (aged 4).

It was a few years later that my mum remarried to a man named Chris Raymond. I was one of the lucky ones that would now have two dads to look after me. I was also fortunate enough to also gain a brother in this union. Cam was 11 months younger than me, and based on custody arrangements, he also lived with us. He became my new little mate and we were together 24/7. Cam was also a witness to my strange little rituals, and until much later in life, he didn't really think twice about them.

They were just what I did.

I truly believe I grew up with an undiagnosed, untreated anxiety condition, but in those days, a parent taking their child to a psychologist for assessment was not common unless there were serious consequences from unusual behaviour.

I was generally always fearful of "something". I suffered terribly from nightmares and always seemed to be acutely aware of the things I thought I needed to worry about.

I remember when I was nine, running to my mum in full panic mode, tears streaming down my face because I had suddenly thought to myself, "What if my mum *now* is not my mum in heaven?"

The overthinking and Obsessive Compulsive Disorder-like thoughts were well and truly part of my DNA and, at times, ruled the way I behaved. I would wake up each morning and my first thought was: *"What do I need to worry about today?"* At night, I had to have my teddies lined up perfectly, and before I went to bed, I would kick my foot behind the opened bedroom door three times to make sure there was nothing scary behind it. On a bad day, this would be repeated several times. It was as though my brain didn't trust my eyes.

This kind of routine was always exacerbated when I was stressed. A little strange, but a tell-tale sign of what was to come later in life, especially when there were adult responsibilities involved.

Ironically, from the outside looking in, I was a confident, outgoing, and outspoken little personality. I never suffered from social anxiety, quite the opposite, which I now believe to be the reason why my mental health issues flew under everyone's radar for many, many years. My nan would take me into the nursing home to see my great grandmother. Within minutes, I would have all the residents gathered in the recreation hall and I would become the entertainment for the afternoon.

As a girl, I would literally put on a show for anyone who would watch and was renowned for quickly coordinating a routine with my brother and throwing an impromptu performance on whatever platform was available. I thrived in an environment where I was able to express myself.

I found freedom in music and the arts and quickly became drawn to singing, dancing, and entertaining. I attended lessons in these disciplines from the age of five, and being an entertainer was all I could think about. From the time I can remember, that was all I wanted to do. Put me in front of a camera and it was on. I came alive with confidence and my thoughts became a whole lot quieter. Singing would later become my professional career from my late teens to late 20s.

In 1981, at the age of eight and a half, my family decided we were going to move north to Queensland's Gold Coast. My step-dad had already secured work designing large housing developments and that was going to set us up nicely. This would prove to be a highly beneficial move for everyone, but at the time, all I could see was that the rest of my family were further away. My mum was pregnant with my soon-to-be little sister, Cassie, who was born within weeks, arriving in January 1982. She became my much-needed distraction and an opportunity for me to play the role of mum.

The checking and over-checking continued but the focus shifted towards my sister. Every evening before bed, I would go over to her cot (and later bed) and put my hand on her chest to feel if she was breathing. If I happened to wake up through the night, I could not fall back to sleep until I had checked her again, and not indifferent to kicking behind my door, I would do this several times if I was a little more out of sorts than usual.

The compulsion to confirm her wellbeing also overrode any remote fear I had of the dark.

OCD

According to the current edition of the Diagnostic and Statistical Manual of Mental Disorders (DSM-V), Obsessive compulsive disorder (OCD) is an intrusive involuntary condition consisting of unwanted, recurrent and persistent, thoughts urges or images (obsessions) that cause profound anxiety or distress.

The affected person tries to 'neutralise' or suppress the obsessive thoughts, urges or images with another thought or action (the compulsion). Compulsions are typically performed repetitively.

Compulsive behaviours might comprise hand washing, checking, or placing things in certain orders. Compulsive mental acts include silently praying, counting, or repeating certain words. The person feels driven to perform these acts in response to the obsession, often according to rules that must be rigidly adhered to.

The function of the compulsion is to reduce anxiety or prevent a feared event or situation, even though the connection between the action and the feared situation is frequently unrealistic.

Dr Tamar Chansky asserts that no one is to blame for OCD. Essentially, a part of the brain that 'filters' information malfunctions; thoughts and beliefs that would otherwise be forgotten become 'stuck'. Although sufferers appear to choose to control their environments by imposing, for example, order, cleanliness, or symmetry, in reality the person is "trapped by an unrelenting heckler who throws out jabs of worry, fear, and uncertainty, making it impossible to take things for granted". The thoughts generated are involuntary "junk mail" from the brain. Unfortunately, the OCD-sufferer increasingly reads and responds to the junk mail at the expense of useful, adaptive messages (thoughts).

Chansky, T. E. (2000). Freeing your child from obsessive-compulsive disorder.

New York, US: Three Rivers Press

Mum and Dad's (Chris) wedding day 1980.

My new little mate and brother, Cam.

And then there was five of us with the arrival of baby
sister, Cassie.

Always looking over my little sister.

As a teen, I worried about all of the usual things a teenage girl would worry about. *"Am I pretty enough? Where do I fit in? Will I have the career of my dreams? What if I don't pass my exams?"* These questions were on my mind often, but with a little bit more intensity than the average person, I suspect.

Again I found comfort in the arts and my music. I performed in all of our school and community shows and volunteered regularly to be the subject of any photography student portfolio.

I felt totally safe in that space and the focus that required allowed me to be free from my own thoughts, even just momentarily.

My introduction to alcohol was nothing out of the ordinary for a high schooler. My first drink was at a friend's party in 1989 on the Gold Coast when I was 16 and the drink of choice was West Coast Coolers, an almost soft-drink-tasting alcohol that provided a little happy kick. I had a wonderful group of friends that looked out for each other, including my first boyfriend, Milo Gaffney. He was a protector and an all-round nice guy who I remember fighting hard to win over. Tall, blonde, and handsome and a typical Gold Coast surfer dude who was two years older than me. I was pretty smitten, and with a little convincing, I managed to make my way to becoming his 'girlfriend'.

Although drinking was not frequent as a young adult, it certainly had my attention. Under the influence, I was a little bit more confident, less inhibited, and my nervous thoughts were dulled.

The relationship with Milo and I ran its course and it was not long afterwards at the age of 16 that I met the boyfriend who would make me unstuck, Michael Szumowski. I was in my final year of school at Miami High and he was a member of highly successful late 1980s/early 90s Australian pop-rock band, *Indecent*

Obsession. My best friend, Louise, introduced me to him in a 'double date' scenario with her and her boyfriend at the time, David Dixon, who was the lead singer of the band. We hit it off instantly and I fell madly and deeply in love. He was everything I had dreamed of and ticked all the boxes and a whole lot more. He also had an innate way of making me feel safe, secure, and less fearful of the future. With him, I always felt like I was in a really good place.

Unfortunately, our relationship was always fraught by distance. The band travelled a lot both domestically and internationally. I remember so much of this time pining for him to be home. We would have endless conversations over the phone from overseas that resulted in ginormous telephone bills. We would also send letters—real old-fashioned pen on paper letters—and constantly counted down the days until we would be back together again.

During this time, I was given an opportunity to sing with the band as a backing vocalist, performing with them all over Australia. This included supporting our very own pop princess, Kylie Minogue, on her first Australian tour and appearing on several mainstream television shows such as 'Hey Hey it's Saturday' and 'Countdown Revolution'. At the age of 16 I flew solo to Los Angeles to meet the band who were filming their latest music clip in the California desert. Michael and I then flew over to London to see Prince live at Wembley Arena and on to Paris for a few days of exploring. Seriously, an unforgettable experience for someone so young and all of this while I was still completing my Year 12 High School studies.

It felt like a dream.

And maybe that was the start of the problem.

Michael and I clicked on so many levels and I wholeheartedly believed at the time that he was 'the one'.

But it all came crashing down when I turned 18. We had moved down to Melbourne together so I could commence my own music career and he would be closer to the record company and media. In one swift kick, he dumped me over the telephone, claiming it wasn't going to work out because he was spending too much time away with the band, which by then had based themselves in Los Angeles. (1991). But at a later date, I became acutely aware that I had probably been one of many other women in his life during that time.

Just another large tug at the already frayed heartstrings.

My world fell apart in an instant. I had never known heartbreak like that before, and I could not see myself moving through the pain.

Welcome, destructive behaviour.

My drinking sessions were no longer fun and light-hearted. They became opportunities to forget my sadness and hide my pain.

Over the next few months, I partied a little harder than usual, and whilst under the influence, I made a lot more 'loose' decisions. Late nights, a few impromptu hook-ups with other guys, which always followed with huge regret; something that exacerbated the anxiety that was starting to make its way to the surface.

I was constantly trying to escape from the torture of not having him in my life.

One night, I was house-sitting for a family friend and I was on the phone with Michael. Stupidly, but true to my vulnerability in his presence, I'd hooked up with him briefly on one of his trips home from LA. At the time, I was willing to take anything he gave me, including casual sex. But it was on this *one* phone call that he said in no uncertain terms that what we had was over and he didn't want any more casual encounters.

The finality of those words, after holding a fiercely burning flame for him for so long, hit me like a ton of bricks.

Years later, through counselling, this was identified as being another key factor in my internal belief that I needed to be "more" to be loved—to be perfect in every way.

But on that night, I was on my own in that house.

I was alone with my pain.

I was by myself with my thoughts and I could not cope with the overwhelming feeling of emptiness.

I went to the kitchen, grabbed two beers from the fridge, and took them to bed with me. I sculled both and lay there waiting for the numbness to kick in. And eventually, it did. All the hurt, all the pain, all the tears. They all stopped existing for just a brief period.

That night, my relationship with alcohol changed. It became medication.

The frequent 'goodbyes' at the airport.

On stage with David Dixon from Indecent Obsession.
(1990)

Melbourne Tennis Centre (now Rod Laver Arena) Kylie
Minogue tour January 1990.

Experiencing London in 1990 at the age of 16.

Michael and I on 'set' in Los Angeles.

Over the next few years, I continued with my music career, working and travelling the world. Just before I turned 19, I signed a contract to perform in a Madonna tribute show in Japan and found myself completely out of my comfort zone. I was away from home in a foreign country and suddenly being exposed to the world of Japanese style men-only bars. This was the first time in my life I felt like I was being treated simply as a 'pound of flesh', which just didn't sit well with me.

Anxiety was high and, again, alcohol helped me cope. There were endless bottles of spirits in the change rooms that belonged to individual customers and it was not uncommon for me to take quick swigs of whiskey and cognac before and during show time. In fact, it became habitual. This curbed my nerves and gave me more confidence to step onto the stage and perform. And just like an extra set of steak knives, the bonus was that I forgot about my broken heart for another brief moment.

Drinking continued to ease the heartache from the torch I still held for Michael which lasted years.

When I returned to my Burleigh Heads home from Japan in 1992, I entered a relationship with a man who was a non-drinker and focused on fitness. For the next two years, alcohol was almost non-existent in my life. Although this partnership was far from ideal, in so many ways, it served me well. It gave me an introduction to the benefits of exercise and kept me away from the drink.

We moved to Melbourne in 1994 so I could pursue my music career and, in doing so, I moved away from my family on the Gold Coast, which proved to be detrimental in upcoming years. I had no idea how much I was going to need their support.

Eight months later, this relationship came to its inevitable end… and that's when the doors of opportunity opened up for me. I was knee-deep in my music in Melbourne, surrounding myself with like-minded people and ultimately scored a recording deal with Sony Music with my pop group, *Eclipse*, which was literally formed in a café on Brunswick Street, Fitzroy through a friend of a friend.

My girlfriend, Renee, had made acquaintances with a music manager named Jaime Jimenez who was already managing another group at the time named Culture Shock. The aim was to merge the two groups and pitch this to Sony Records. Within a few months, both of these things happened and before I knew it, we were signed to Sony and about to release our first single.

This led to more of what I loved the most—photoshoots, video clips, television appearances, and stage performances. My happy place. Along with this came a bucket load of industry pressure to look good, sound good, and perform well—something that my dreaded anxiety thrived on.

While I loved these aspects, I also crumbled with fear about not living up to everyone's expectations, again reinforcing that voice inside my head telling me I was not good enough… I must be better, even perfect.

The ideal environment for my Obsessive Compulsive Disorder to start rearing its ugly head.

I began to focus on minimalizing my calories wherever I could and not in a healthy way, just so it was assured that I would be able to squeeze into whatever garment the stylists wanted to dress me in. It was also not uncommon for me to 'purge' my food after eating if there were feelings of guilt associated.

Over the next two years (1995-96), I played the game. *Eclipse* gave me a Top 20 hit single, *The Look of Love*, which included releases in Europe, numerous television and magazine appearances, networking opportunities and, more importantly, a load of belly laughs with people I still hold friendships with today. There was a sense of deep understanding that we were all in this together, even if our drivers were different, and for me, there was safety in that. Alcohol was present, but it was much more of a social thing then. It did, however, help me relax and take the edge off of things like performance nerves.

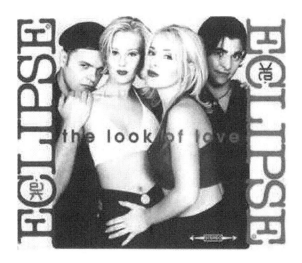

Our first single, 'The Look of Love'.

Our second single, 'In the name of love'.

Grabs from the music video for 'The look of love'.

Through a friend of the band, I met the man who would become my first husband, whom I will refer to throughout this book as Mr X.

The beginning of this relationship was full of immense passion and perhaps some infatuation. He was handsome, charismatic, but very mysterious. Swept up in the love and romance, I was blindsided to flaws in his behaviour, which led to dark holes in our marriage. He kept an awful lot to himself and liked to party, often going out at night and not returning until the next morning. There was a lot of secretive behaviour that would later be brought out in the open.

In 1997, the dynamics in *Eclipse* and, to a larger degree, within the management team, were unsettled and definitely not focused in a positive way. There was no clear direction and everyone involved had a different opinion on how the future should pan out.

In between all of this, my relationship with Mr X was deteriorating. I suspected there was a lot of things he was keeping from me and my anxiety soared sky-high. Panic attacks were occurring daily and, in turn, I upped the participation in the social drinking scene and also started bringing a bottle of wine home at night. Even when by myself, this was now a common occurrence. I'd open the bottle when I walked in of an evening and fell into the habit of taking one last glass to bed with me. On the odd occasion, I would fall asleep before I had drunk it and wake in the morning to the wreaking smell of wine right next to the bed.

I decided to quit the group at the end of 1997. I needed space to breathe without feeling like every move I made was being judged. I wanted a break from the spotlight and, more importantly, an opportunity to focus on my crumbling relationship.

But one night soon after, we had another one of the volatile arguments that I had started to become accustomed to. I can't remember the exact reasons behind the conflict and I quickly learnt the art of blocking it all out.

The most distressing part of this is that when it was all over, I was begging him not to leave.

In hindsight, I should have seen that coming, but true to someone in love, you will overlook the inevitable when you don't want to believe it's 'your' truth.

And, of course, I told *nobody*.

However, the next day, I made a phone call to a friend that was living in Canada and about to travel around Europe. I also spoke to my close girlfriend in London.

So, disillusioned and a little desperate, I packed my bags and took off for London. The next few months were filled with incredible travel experiences I will cherish forever… along with a lot of alcohol. I used it to party, ease the nerves of meeting new people, and even pass the time on long train rides from country to country. All whilst being able to be disguised as 'social inclusion' on a trip of a lifetime.

Once again, it had crept back into my life as the most reliable source of escape.

I was also still in love and desperately wanted to be back with Mr X and to be given an opportunity to '*fix*' things. I felt it was my responsibility.

If I am different, better, more perfect, things will be better; he will be better.

After numerous phone calls from overseas telephone boxes on foreign city street corners, Mr X gave me the news that I had been waiting to hear.

He wanted me back.

So, diligently, I made the travel arrangements and got myself back home as soon as I could.

A red in the piazza in Madrid.

The mini red train 'travellers'.

I fell in love with Florence on this trip.

A moment of reflection in Paris.

Amongst the 'grapes' that I loved so much in Saint Emillion.

When I arrived, our relationship went full steam ahead. It was as if we picked up exactly where we left off; the good, the bad, and of course, the ugly. We moved in together and it was only 12 months before we became engaged. We married in 1999, bought our first home that year, and by July 2001, I was pregnant with my firstborn, Evelyn Grace, who was born in April 2002.

At that point, alcohol for me went back to strictly 'social', and during my pregnancy, I did not drink at all. That was until significant cracks started appearing in my already fraught relationship.

Volatile moments like the one before I took off for Europe had been a regular occurrence over these years but the deeper I got, the harder it was to leave. In 2003, things became so fractured that we sought marriage counselling. I was desperate for this to work out and I think I would have done just about anything for him to ensure that we kept the 'family unit' together as I had always envisaged.

Ironically, it was during one of those sessions that he disclosed to the counsellor about one of the affairs he had recently had. At the time, this vital message was not passed on to me at the advice of the counsellor but would eventually come to the surface at a later date.

In hindsight, I somehow managed to shoulder the blame for this also.

"I shouldn't have said that", "I could have been more supportive", "If only I had been more attentive". In fact, the amount of responsibility I took for his unhappiness and subsequent 'faux pas' (plural) was ludicrous.

But just like many in these kinds of relationships, I wanted to believe that it was me that could make everything better.

And so, it was in late February 2004 that my little man, Wilson, was conceived and later born in the November of that year. I for one was hoping that the birth of this new little joyous spirit would bring the changes to our marriage I had longed for.

But on all accounts, it just got worse.

To add to this, I was spending copious hours in the evenings by myself whilst Mr X was out at friends' houses almost seven nights per week. Whilst Wilson slept, my darling three-year-old, Evie, would sit with me on the couch and watch soap operas that distracted me from my current life. She was so loving and sensitive and was without a doubt the reason that I was still putting one foot in front of the other. Both of my angels were.

But I was so lonely, I felt unloved, unheard, neglected, and unwanted, so I welcomed back that familiar warm and fuzzy feeling that alcohol had previously given me.

Those close to me know the details intimately of the 10 years we were together and the extraordinary lengths I went to in order to regain any resemblance of self-worth, self-confidence, and self-respect. I had conditioned myself to morph into whatever was needed to keep the peace for so long, I lost my own identity. Every ounce of confidence in my personal abilities was destroyed.

I truly believe this was the exact point where I became disconnected from my soul.

I was beginning to make decisions that did not align with my better judgment or morals purely out of desperation to feel some remote sense of happiness.

We eventually separated on mutual terms in March 2006, and with a four-year-old daughter and 15-month-old son to look after on my own, I kicked into survival mode to ensure they were well cared for. This was always my priority, even when I was drinking to block out the pain.

But in the few weeks prior to Mr X moving out of our home, I had been drinking heavily. The enormity of what was about to occur in terms of my livelihood, the eventual sale of my home, and the disintegration of the family unit suddenly became overbearing.

In the mornings, I was sneaking in a swig of vodka and topping myself up throughout the day. I had even resorted to hiding it in empty shampoo bottles in the bathroom cabinet for when I needed to calm the nerves quickly on the sly.

Late one afternoon, I started to get the sweats and my heart was racing a million miles per hour. I felt like I was going to have a heart attack and the panic was overwhelming. At the time, I thought I needed medical attention for the anxiety, so I called my uncle who lived nearby and asked him to take me to the hospital.

I was terrified.

I remember calling my parents in Queensland in the car on the way and telling them that I believed I needed to be admitted to hospital for a while, purely to get control of the anxiety.

Upon arriving in the hospital, I disclosed to the triage nurse what had been going on. They performed all of their usual observations and checks and it was determined that, physically, I was fine.

That in itself calmed me right down.

The doctors then took me through to another room where I was greeted by a social worker that, by all accounts, was just a really lovely, calm, and compassionate man.

After describing the last few months and subsequent weeks of alcohol intake, he then proceeded to tell me that what I was experiencing was actually withdrawal symptoms for the excessive drinking.

I think my jaw actually hit the floor.

It was the first time that I had experienced 'detox-like' symptoms to this extent, so much so that he recommended for the next few days I take measured doses of Valium to get things back under control. This would also reduce my overall anxiety and allow my nervous system a reprieve.

My uncle drove me back home and, already, with the first dose of medication, I was feeling a lot more stable, but just deeply and desperately sad.

As the months passed after our separation, my loneliness led me to look for some company and I registered myself on to an online dating site, hoping to meet a man that was the complete opposite to what I'd had in my marriage.

And that is exactly what happened.

My first date with David, an industry company executive, was on my 33rd birthday at Kuni's Japanese restaurant in the city. I remember waiting for him to pick me up from my home, and at this point, we had only talked over the phone. To muster up some liquid courage, I downed a glass or two of champagne in the lead up to his arrival. When I opened the door and realized he looked just like his picture online, in fact, more handsome, I was quietly relieved. To add to my delight, he wanted to have a drink before we left which gave me another opportunity to get one more in before dinner.

The date was so comfortable and exciting. We laughed a LOT! He made me feel like I was someone special for the first time in years and, almost instantly, I felt 'safe' when I was with him.

In the coming weeks, he took me on drives to the country, dinners out at nice restaurants, he cooked beautiful meals for me at home, bought me thoughtful gifts, but mostly just showed up as a decent, kind, and morally-driven human being.

Over time, our relationship flourished, our friendship manifested into love, and we eventually moved in together into a Box Hill home in Melbourne's east… children and all.

We became engaged in mid-2008 and were married on March 26, 2009, at the beautiful 1885 heritage-listed Butleigh Wootten mansion in Kew, famous for its magnificent weddings and receptions. It was everything I could have asked for and more. Evie and Wilson walked me down the aisle and handed me over to the man that had welcomed us all into his arms.

My parents openly expressed their happiness and gratitude on this day in their speeches for the man that had scooped up their little girl and grandchildren and provided them with the love and support they both deserved and needed.

He won everyone's heart and had stolen mine.

David understood and accepted me for who I was and helped me heal and become whole again, but not before a few more years of self-sabotage.

My two most precious people walked me down the aisle
and gave me away.

The man that stole my heart.

The kids and David became unseparable.

In the next few years that followed, I had periods when I felt in control, but mostly, I was drowning in post-traumatic stress and grief for the life I thought I would have. Financially, I was starting all over again, and emotionally, I had been ripped apart. The children were so young and passing them back and forth in a custody arrangement I had not properly thought through when signing, was just another tick on the "reason to drink" list.

When I met David, I was broken but he gave me glimmers of hope that life could be good again and I was worthy of love just as I was. He took on the kids as if they were his own and provided me with the stability I had longed for on so many levels.

However, the problem was that he also liked a drink.

Our home and social life revolved around drinking… so my little secret could be easily disguised. I would drink what was out in the open because it was acceptable between us and then I would drink from the bottle that I had hidden in the wardrobe or underneath my bed. We would indulge each other regularly, which left no opportunity to address what was clearly becoming a big issue.

Even fishing at the beach required a drink.

David was playing exactly the same card.

Health was not a priority for either of us.

At David's 40th birthday party.

On August 11, 2009, Evie came home from her father's place with what I thought was a urinary tract infection. She had been urinating excessively for days and had wet the bed twice that weekend. In hindsight, I remembered in the weeks prior she had gone to bed at 7 pm and by 7.30 pm, she was either going to the toilet or at the kitchen sink drinking water almost catatonically. She had also dropped a little bit of weight.

As I had to get antibiotics for a tooth infection that morning, I took Evie along with me to my doctor's clinic and I innocently thought she would only require a course herself and she would be okay. Within 15 minutes, our entire life changed. One simple urine sample and a finger prick test and she was diagnosed with type 1 diabetes.

The doctor explained that the excessive urinating and subtle weight loss that she had been experiencing were all prominent symptoms of her diagnosis.

We were urgently ushered to the Emergency Department of the Melbourne Royal Children's Hospital. The doctor wanted her to go in an ambulance, but I was insistent we drive her ourselves. It was the most surreal experience I have ever had.

My beautiful little seven-year-old girl sat in the back of the car looking nervous and wondering what on earth was happening. David was driving, I was in the front passenger seat, and looking at her, I had no real idea what this was going to mean for her and us. I did, however, have some knowledge about type 1 diabetes and knew that her life was about to become very different because there is no cure.

Thinking about that moment in time to this day still makes me well up with tears.

It wasn't until years later that I could even bring myself to look at photos of her pre-diagnosis. Carefree and happy without the responsibilities of being a diabetic.

But whilst Evie took on this new challenge with gusto, I didn't. Everything felt like it was spiralling out of control. My drinking patterns were much more "medicating" and a whole lot less social. And I was still mostly disguising my intake.

I'd gained a lot of weight over the last few years and that familiar alcoholic flushed face and bloat was super evident. My body constantly covered in unexplained bruises due to my low platelet count. My wardrobe started to consist of baggy, unflattering clothing and anything that I felt 'comfortable' in.

I absolutely HATED how I looked and I despised even more who I had become.

A woman with no identity.

A woman who had lost control.

A woman who had no purpose.

A woman who had lost her soul.

The kids were going back and forth with their father and I was beginning to get feedback that they were unhappy with the arrangement. This deepened the conflict between him and I, which, in turn, exacerbated my anxiety and increased my desire to drink.

And drink I did.

I was slowly slipping away from being a functional alcoholic to a non-functioning one.

In Vanuatu for my Mum's 60th January 2011.

My weight was at an all time high and so was my anxiety.

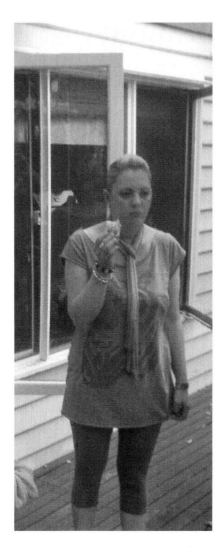

My body and face were bloated and toxic.

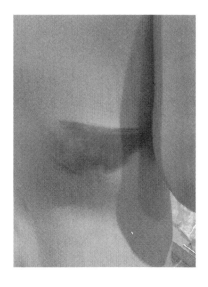

Unexplainable bruises all over my body.

I had psoriasis for years due to the toxity in my blood.

CHAPTER 1

I'M NOT HER ANYMORE

BY THE END of 2011, I was so far in my own mess that my vision beyond some 40cm was blurred. I was completely lost in my screwed-up, numbed-out world with a body that was slowly dying on me.

I was self-medicating day and night and spending my days getting through minute-by-minute, fighting addiction and depression. I could no longer pretend I had one ounce of control.

It was gone.

I was still living in Melbourne with David and the kids, but without the support of my family who were back in my hometown on the Gold Coast. Life was unmanageable.

On weekdays, I would feed the kids breakfast, drive them to school, then return home and down a couple of glasses of wine so I could feel calm enough to sleep. My alarm would go off at 1 pm so I had enough time to put dinner together, do the washing, prepare Evie's insulin doses, and trust that the evening would run smoothly.

Then would come the trip to school for the afternoon pick-up, or if I was feeling "under the weather", I had a few school mums who would drop the kids home for me. For this, I will be forever grateful.

I would spend the next few hours just sitting with them watching movies, reading stories, and generally just holding them tight. My two precious children were the only things remotely keeping me together.

I would then have a couple of glasses of wine before they went to bed, but the real dosing came after they were asleep. But before that happened, I would once again prepare for the morning. Lunches were made, uniforms were neatly placed out, Evie's morning insulin dose drawn up, and the schoolbags packed.

I cared about nothing else in the world but them.

In Melbourne, I had no real family support. My dad (Don) lived a few hours away, and by all accounts, he was trying to support me as best as he could. And of all people, he knew the tell-tale signs of someone in deep trouble with alcohol addiction.

Let me fill you in.

My dad had been sober at that point for almost 24 years. Albeit, I don't remember this being part of my early childhood, my dad's affiliation with problem-drinking had already commenced when I was a young girl. In fact, he found 'courage' in the liquid during his late teens. Much like myself, alcohol for him was more purposeful for its mind-altering properties than its favourable taste.

This continued past the separation with my mum and through his second marriage until, one day, he reached his very own rock bottom and surrendered. Alcoholics Anonymous was his pathway to recovery and that was where he found solace and support.

As you can imagine, there were several poignant and heart-breaking moments for him whilst he observed his only child slowly being taken away from him in the same manner he almost lost himself, and sometimes this was just too much for him to bear.

And today, I get that.

Nobody really knew what to do next, my dad included.

It was during a brief visit to see my family on the Gold Coast, with some twisting of my arm, that I made a decision that the kids and I needed to move there, even if it was only temporary. It was not meticulously thought through and David didn't have any idea of how this was going to work for him and his job based in Melbourne.

Our relationship was showing deep cracks at that time due to the unpredictability of my drinking and constant poor state of health. There was no certainty of anything other than the fact that I knew I needed help and the children needed to be around family.

Upon return to Melbourne, I started to pack up our belongings, along with my life, and with a lot of assistance, the kids and I made our way back to the place I had not called home for almost 20 years: Burleigh Heads.

There was no real excitement, just a deep sense of relief that some of the pressure to hold it all together would be gone and my parents and siblings, Cassie and Cam, would take some of the load.

Even though my head was far from clear, something deep down in my soul told me I was doing the right thing… that this was going to be my healing. I truly believe it's the hardest decisions that are generally the right ones. It's like the Big Man upstairs rewards us for being so brave. And for me, this turned out to be true.

I arrived home in December 2011 and let all of my guards down. Ironically, when I was finally in the safety of my family, my psychological and physical state worsened, not helped one iota by the drinking. It was as though I finally felt like I could take my foot off the pedal knowing I had extra help with the kids. David stayed in Melbourne to continue with his work and was commuting back and forth to the Gold Coast as often as he could.

Everything was so real, so raw, so intense. I just wanted to curl up and die.

There are a couple of incidences that almost cost me my life and my parents and Cassie were thankfully there to rescue me.

Much of my drinking was "hidden" from them, or so I thought. I was being watched like a hawk so I was sneaking it in whenever and wherever I could. I would venture to the local bottle shop and buy miniature bottles of vodka so I could stash them in secret places. It felt like "the perfect crime". The only problem was that I had to dispose of the bottles somehow, and that proved to be tricky. I'd collect them all in a plastic bag and hide them until I had an opportunity to dump them in a public bin. I distinctly remember the feeling of sheer relief when they were finally in the rubbish, and for that moment, that time around, I had not been caught.

And in complete desperation, I even resorted to taking swills from bottles of alcohol-based mouthwash. I knew how dangerous this was but I took the risk anyway.

Something my memory will never erase.

For someone who had never been able to lie and loathes deceit, alcoholism created a persona that I despised. The shame was awful, but the guilt was so much worse and drove me to drink even more.

One particular morning, after an evening of knocking myself out, I woke up once again feeling like death. My skin felt like it was crawling with bugs, my heart was racing, the panic was overwhelming, and the detox tremors were insane. My face was still black from a fall a few days earlier that I barely remembered.

Evie and Wilson had been taken to school by my parents who then took off to Sydney for a weekend break. God knows they needed it after a month with me.

Cassie was due to pick me up at 9 am so the kids and I could spend the weekend with her. I was not to be left alone, but the thought of getting through the next few hours feeling the way I did was unbearable. I went into the lounge room and raided my step-dad's alcohol cabinet and poured a little from each bottle into a big tumbler glass, hoping nobody would notice. I went back for seconds, then thirds. I believe in about the space of 30 minutes, I had downed around 500ml of straight spirits.

Arriving at Cassie's home, I went to the spare bedroom because I just needed to sleep. The next thing I remember was waking up in an ambulance on the way to Robina Hospital and trying to answer the paramedic's questions about how much I had drunk. Cassie had called my GP who advised her to call 000, quoting an ambulance code specific to my critical inebriated state.

The pressure I put on my family is something I am still ashamed of and feel extremely guilty for. For heaven's sake, my sister had a six-month-old baby boy and in order to go to the hospital with me, she had quickly arranged for her neighbour to look after him. But at that point, I was completely unaware of the repercussions of my actions and that included what I had just done to myself.

Apart from the large volume of spirits, medical staff also thought the Valium I had taken overnight was playing part of the story. I was admitted to the emergency ward with a blood-alcohol level of 0.38%, a platelet count of around 16, and my GGT liver function was over 2000.

I was in real trouble.

They kept me in the emergency department for eight hours and the comedown was horrendous. I didn't want the kids to see any of that, so family members arranged for me to be accommodated overnight in the short-stay ward where I detoxed under supervision for the next crucial 24 hours.

I was visited by the mental health team and asked many questions to establish how critical I was. "*Do you want to harm yourself? Have you ever thought of committing suicide? What family support do you have? Have you tried a rehabilitation program?*" I can still see their concerned faces staring at me. My answers were simply "*yes/no*" and were muttered through a waterfall of tears.

All I wanted was to be back with my babies and for it to all go away.

Unbeknown to me, my parents had contacted David and he quickly booked a flight from Melbourne. He arrived with Cassie at the hospital that afternoon and I was discharged with strict instructions about how to manage my next few days of detox with Valium. I hung my head in shame on the drive home, hardly spoke, and started the cycle of resentment for those who were trying to stop me from getting what I wanted—another drink.

David stayed with me for a few days before returning to Melbourne for work. When he was with me, I not only had less opportunity to sneak a drink, but I also felt less inclined to. His presence gave the glimmer of hope I needed to get back on my feet. But after he left, I fell apart again.

I went a few days without drinking and moped around the house like a bear with a sore head, but it wasn't long before I caved in again and found ways to slip in sly ones. My parents were meticulous in shielding Evie and Wilson from the dire straits I was in. As far as they were aware, Mum was just very tired and a little unwell.

One afternoon, my mum was unable to arouse me fully from a nap and I ended up back in hospital, despite my protests. The mental health team assessed me as non-critical despite me going through the detox tremors. My mum wanted me to stay in hospital but I argued incessantly with her until, finally, we all went home. I am assuming the doctors gave them some directive as to what to do with me afterwards, but all I knew was I just wanted to go to bed.

My dad (Don) had flown up from Melbourne and there was a family meeting about the right course of action, not only for me but also for them. My dad said that if he had seen me in the street at this time, he would not have recognized me, his own daughter.

I was an absolute mess.

Detoxing haze makes time feel distorted and irrelevant, but during the next few weeks, I was shipped between the Gold Coast homes of my sister, my brother, and my parents for 24/7 watch, so the kids had constant care with my family, screened from a deeply troubled and terribly unwell mother.

My GP insisted I go into a private rehabilitation program as my situation was now critical. Reluctantly, I agreed, but at that point, simply to get everyone off my back. I was so deep in my own despair that I did not know which way was up and which way was down.

It was decided I would not have to be an in-patient at the Currumbin Rehab Clinic, but instead, to attend the day program twice a week for two months. But it was made clear in no uncertain terms that if I did not attend or participate fully, I would be going in to stay.

But in the same breath that I displayed vexation for this intervention, I also inhaled a sense of peace that I had not experienced in some time. Deep down, I acknowledged I was in way over my head and there was no way I could do this on my own.

I know now this was my very own surrender.

David and I at my best friend's wedding in March 2012. This is probably the only photograph taken during my absolute worst period. I didn't allow cameras and to be honest, no-one wanted to photograph me anyway. At this point I had probably hit 48kgs.

Treating Physician

Dr EPM Fisser

B.Pharm, MBBCh, MRCGP (UK), FRACGP

PRE-DETOX

Justine first came to my rooms in January 2012 as a vastly different human being than she is today.

In the grip of her alcoholism, Justine was agitated, defensive, introverted, and suffered from agoraphobia which limited her to leaving the house only to buy alcohol. This led to endless lonely days and nights and did nothing to improve her extreme mood swings.

Physically, Justine was dishevelled. Her hair was lacklustre, her face drawn and her skin was dull and lifeless. With the vast majority of her calories coming from alcohol, her emaciated 47kg frame could only be described as anorexic.

Managing a patient with alcoholism requires a thorough understanding of what is going on inside the body and blood tests are an important diagnostic tool.

Tell-tale signs of excessive alcohol abuse are elevated gamma-glutamyl transferase (GGT), mean cell volume (MCV), triglycerides, and platelets.

1. GGT is a liver enzyme that breaks down alcohol. It is elevated in those who abuse alcohol because more is required to metabolise alcohol toxins.

2. MCV is a measure of the average size of a patient's red blood cells. Red blood cells carry oxygen from the lungs to every cell in the body. If they are too large, they don't function properly. This is usually a result of alcohol abuse.

3. Triglycerides - Alcohol contains an excessive amount of sugar. It can increase both your bad cholesterol and triglycerides by impeding the body's ability to break down fat because the liver is too busy breaking down alcohol.

4. Decreased Platelets - Platelets are import for clotting of blood. Alcohol abuse may impact the shape and function of platelets, leading to bruising.

When diagnosing alcohol abuse, the combination of GGT and MCV is the most important combination of tests.

The first step in managing a patient suffering from alcoholism is the dreaded DETOX.

In detox, the patient completely stops drinking. This is no easy process and has a number of challenging hurdles to overcome. Symptoms usually start at 6-7 hours. These include behavioural changes—anxiety, agitation, irritability, hallucinations, a physical tremor, and even seizures. It is an extremely dangerous process and, in some cases, can prove fatal. A patient in detox must, therefore, be carefully and continuously monitored by medical professionals in a clinical setting.

My Sobriety Step 1

- Assess your *real* relationship with alcohol.

- How long can you go without it and why do you need it?

- Reach out to a friend, family member, or support group and tell them your truth.

- Admit to yourself that you can't do this on your own and then create a solid plan.

- Find a safe space and place that will allow your transition to occur.

- Be open to the fact that life has to look different for a little while.

- Establish your 'why' and put it at the forefront of every decision.

Actually, I just woke up one day and decided I didn't want to feel like that anymore, or ever again, so I changed.

~ Author unknown.

Chapter 2

DIDN'T WANNA GO TO REHAB

I STARTED attending clinic workshops that focused on strategies to manage my mental health and, more importantly, to try to understand what it was that was driving the need for me to drink my way out of my misery.

I did what was required of me by staff and family, but believe me, I wasn't a willing participant. I longed for the days to be over so I could go home, hold my babies, take my medication, and go to sleep. It really was a case of going through the motions and there were days my parents had to push me to stay with the recovery program.

There were nights at home when I drank undetected and paid for it the next morning, so much so that I begged my parents not to make me attend the clinic. My family were doing their best to help me get well, but I had little regard for their support at that stage. It was all about me... me, me, me. Me and my own pain.

Like every progressive step in self-development and healing, there comes a turning point.

About three weeks into the therapy, I woke again with a god-awful hangover and was pleading not to go to rehab. I walked into my parents' office and saw my dad banging his head against the wall showing just how frustrated he was with trying to resolve this all-encompassing dilemma. Albeit, it was a 'gentle' motion, but it indicated just how helpless he was feeling.

That image of him doing that has never left me.

Who the hell was I to put the people who love and care for me through this torment? They were displaying such desperation to get me well and all I could think about was myself.

So, that day I went to the clinic.

On a subconscious level, I knew it was time to get serious, even though I knew this would be the fight of my life. A family member always drove me to the clinic to ensure I actually attended. This day, I sat in my group class with my skin crawling and no access to alcohol, just the Valium I had been prescribed for my withdrawals. I barely participated, which was not unusual as there were days when some people were not in the right mind frame to interact. I think I even napped occasionally.

Nevertheless, that day I decided to be fully part of my recovery, to take in everything that was being given to me in terms of life tools, and it wasn't long before I became a willing participant.

One poignant memory was an art therapy class I attended. We were asked to draw an image of what we felt like now and how we would like to feel in the future. This did not have to be a self-portrait, however, due to my limited art abilities, I decided to draw a picture of what I believed I looked like then and what I wanted to look like.

You might say, "but hang on, they asked you to draw a picture of how you *FELT*, not how you *LOOKED*", but for me, they were one in the same. My present-state impression of myself mirrored what I was feeling on the inside—sadness, dull in colour, hollow cheeks, and emptiness. The future picture depicted me as radiant, flamboyant, happy and colourful—the way I remembered myself many years earlier.

Another group activity in the clinic had a significant impact on me. At about the eight-week mark, we were asked to write some words describing "positively" how we saw other group members. By that stage, we had learnt a lot about each other all through carefully executed therapy.

There was an unspoken rule in the room that judgment was to be thought and not heard. I quickly appreciated the true meaning of this. Even though we were from completely different socio-economic backgrounds, who am I to think I am any different? I may have self-medicated for different reasons through my own traumatic life experiences—and was lucky not to end up on the streets or in a prison—but at the end of the day, as much as it took me a long time to say it, I was an addict just like them.

A bitter pill to swallow but the truth nonetheless.

I know of men and women who try to convince themselves that because they have good jobs, big houses, eat at fancy restaurants, drink expensive wine, and have somewhat stable family lives, their alcoholism is somehow different.

It's not.

They should consider themselves lucky they still have a comfortable lifestyle and the support of people close to them to keep propping them up. But without this support, they have nothing but themselves and their addiction.

At my rehab sessions, I discovered the power of example. After two months of attendances, I had done pretty well. I had managed to almost stop drinking and moved out of my parents' Burleigh Heads home and into a nearby place with the kids. With some serious negotiating by David with the company he was working for at the time, he was given the green light to relocate to the Gold Coast and our relationship was improving.

I started walking the beach daily and was generally functioning well without too much supervision and assistance. I had put on some much-needed weight and I was beginning to look and act like someone who had some degree of clarity and purpose.

The exchanges of favourable comments began at classes. We went around the room and took turns at praising others. I delivered my positivity to each individual and then it came to my turn, the part I most feared. It was time for them to return the favour.

I have never been good at receiving compliments and I still struggle with this.

> *Sometimes I feel words of praise are insincere or I don't believe I deserve them.*

However, my rehab companions said some nice things: "*You are intelligent. I think you are beautiful. I feel supported by you. You're a nice person.*"

But the one that changed my perspective on my journey was: "*Your recovery has given me hope.*"

Six simple words that immediately made me see myself from an angle I had never seen before.

Far out! How did that happen?

From a desperate drunk and out-of-control woman to someone who others were looking up to for some kind of inspiration. Yet, it made me feel good, even though I knew I still had a long way to go.

Natural serotonin and happy hormones were starting to flow through my body and gave me the drive to make positive steps towards my recovery.

Over the years, I had seen several psychologists and other mental health practitioners but had never really experienced the benefits that group therapy gave me. Maybe it was a combination of hitting rock bottom or finally being in an environment where I felt connected, understood, and supported? Maybe it was the sharing, the openness, and the opportunity to lay it all out on the table without fear of repercussion?

I had always responded well to any type of kinaesthetic interaction. Feeling, doing, and being on a level that required emotional commitment and empathy. I definitely know now that I felt much safer among others who were in predicaments similar to mine. But the fear of being alone in my own head can sometimes still be overwhelming.

While attending the clinic, I continued to see my psychologist who reinforced the strategies I was learning and essentially kept me in check. This ticked another box, as far as my family was concerned, in the long list of my maintenance items.

During this time, I was diagnosed with post-traumatic stress disorder, primarily linked to the breakdown of my first marriage. Those 10 years had a significant impact on my self-confidence and what I ultimately thought I was worth.

After the separation in 2006, I spent several years in what was described to me as "survivor mode" where I simply went through the motions of getting myself out, prioritised the kids and financial security, but did not deal with the traumatic impact of the period both during and post my marriage. This manifested into acute anxiety, depression, and ultimately, self-destruction.

With any journey of recovery, every Tom, Dick, and Harry are going to throw in their two-cents' worth of ideas and suggestions about what needs to be done to get well. From suggestions of inpatient treatment to recommendations of medications.

Over the years, I had been put on and off several different anti-depressant/anxiety treatments. I had to stop taking them *all* due to significant side effects ranging from extreme weight loss (one medication caused me to lose 7kg in seven days), spontaneously severe bruising from low platelets, beyond bearable nausea, and constant vomiting.

Shortly before hitting breaking point, I was prescribed another medication that made me go to places in my head that I had never ventured to before. Suicidal thoughts had never been a conscious part of my depression or overall condition. Things were certainly so dark at times that I didn't know how I was ever going to get out, but to consciously take my own life; that had not been on my agenda ever.

There were several occasions, however, that I 'diced with death' purely through lack of judgment and coherence. Alcohol and sedatives can be a deadly combination and it was evident I was pushing that line for a long time.

But on one occasion, at around day six of taking this new anti-depressant, I was driving my car along the highway and I had this overwhelmingly intrusive thought. "What if I swerved my car off the road and into that tree?" It came from left of centre and scared me enough to pull over on the side of the road and call my psychiatrist who quickly demanded that I stop taking the meds and get myself to a safe place surrounded by family.

It has since been discovered I have an inefficient phase two pathway. This is the part of your liver that rids your body of toxins. Mine doesn't seem to clear things as well as it should, therefore, most medications build up in my system to toxicity levels and every side effect that is listed in the warning leaflet, I will inevitably get. So, instead of going on yet another anti-depressant, my specialist decided to keep my medication at Valium, and that seemed to work for me in terms of getting through the withdrawal symptoms for alcohol and temporarily calming down my anxiety.

Most people's intentions when you are in recovery are always good, but their suggestions may not be the right thing for *you*. And as an addict, I know how you can be so desperate to find life on the other side that you are drawn to methods and treatments that may not work. There is definitely not a one-size-fits-all formula for getting your shit together. It literally is trial and error, mostly finding something that you can relate to, that you feel you are growing stronger from and, more importantly, that you can maintain.

As previously mentioned, my dad (Don) had been a long-time devout member of Alcoholics Anonymous. In fact, he has now celebrated more than 33 years of sobriety and still attends weekly AA meetings in Victoria to support the sober community and keep himself in check. Knowing this, I too tried AA meetings a few times while living in Melbourne, but it wasn't quite the right fit for me at the time. I can't really pinpoint why. Maybe it was timing, the format, or even just the fact that I was not ready to give up.

What benefited me the most at that time was a combination of group and one-on-one therapy and the full support of my family.

That was my starting formula.

Then, during a visit to my psychologist, he suggested taking up an exercise program. This would prove to be the most pertinent part of my recovery.

Here came the 'game-changer'.

The self portrait I drew in Art Therapy.
"How I felt and how I wanted to feel".

One of the many cathartic activities in clinic. "Finding your purpose".

FIRST STEP- What you DON'T want in your life

1. Use the blank spaces below, list everything you can think of that cause you anger, stress, frustration, fear, hatred, embarrassment, dissatisfaction of anything that you do not want in your life. Don't think too much about it, just write as many as you can think of.

1. Fear
   Anger
2. Despair
3. Anxiety
4. Panic
   Overwhelmed
   Rushed
5. Out of control feeling
   Disappointment
   Wasted time
   No connections
   Lack of commitment
   No direction
   Lack of purpose
   Emptiness
   Hollow
   Loneliness

SECOND STEP– What you DO want in your life

1. As before, using the blank spaces below, list everything you can think of that you do want in your life. Look back to what your deepest, 'don't wants' tell you about what you really do want. Focus on what makes you happy, fulfilled and satisfied, as well as what gets you energised, motivated and purposeful. Avoid the superficial and the material and go for the deeply satisfying, profoundly rewarding life experiences. Again, don't think too much about it, just write as many as you can:

(1) Contentment
    Joy
    Loved
    Loving others
    connected
(5) Committed
    self disciplined
(3) Healthy me
    Strong
(4) Resilient
    Meaningful
    Enlightened
    Strong family connection
(2) Balanced, Happy kids
    Beautiful husband
    Romance
    passion
    Compassion
    Helping others

feeling valued
sense of greater self worth
belonging
achievements

SECOND STEP– What you DO want in your life

1. As before, using the blank spaces below, list everything you can think of that you do want in your life. Look back to what your deepest, 'don't wants' tell you about what you really do want. Focus on what makes you happy, fulfilled and satisfied, as well as what gets you energised, motivated and purposeful. Avoid the superficial and the material and go for the deeply satisfying, profoundly rewarding life experiences. Again, don't think too much about it, just write as many as you can:

(1) Contentment
Joy
Loved
Loving others
connected
Committed
(5) self assured
(3) Healthy me
Strong
(4) Resilient
Meaningful
Enlightened
Strong family connection
(2) Balanced, Happy kids
Grateful husband
Romance
Passion
Compassion
Helping others

feeling valued
sense of growth/self work
belonging
achievements

FOURTH STEP- Write your own 100th Birthday speech

Years and years from now, after a happy and fulfilling life, you are given the opportunity to write your 100th Birthday speech. **Assuming you have the life that you want from this point forward, what will your 100th Birthday speech say about your life?**

Looking back on the life of

Justine Whitehurst, she stood for many things but none more than the well being & overall happiness of her children. She learnt at the age of 39, that this was not about putting herself last & everyone else first, but exactly the opposite. By being selfless, she was able to give all in her life so much more. She was dedicated to helping everyone around her & her own sense of wellness allowed her to achieve this. It became a role model. Her greatest achievement was taking life on without fear & committing each day to being a better human being.

FIFTH STEP- Put your primary purpose down on paper

Write a very short statement – a phrase, a sentence, no more than a couple of sentences – expressing the essence of what you want about your life to be all about. The acid test for your primary life purpose is your internal barometer. When you write it, you should feel energy, enthusiasm, commitment, a sense of "Yes! This is for me!" If you don't feel this, keep on writing.

The essence of my primary purpose is

to help others by being a selfless, committed & strong, mother, wife, friend, sister, colleague or acquaintance. Demonstrating qualities & behaviours that become a 'model' for others to connect with & help them to find their own purpose in life.

My Sobriety Step 2

- Enrol in a program that suits you and your situation.
- Set up the structure both in and out of the home to commence rehabilitation.
- Take it one day, one minute, or one second at a time.
- Understand you are not going to feel immediate happiness, in fact, sometimes the opposite.
- Tell your loved ones and those close to you how you are feeling at all times.
- Stay in close contact with your doctors.
- Try to be a willing participant but be kind to yourself; this is new.

Rockbottom was the solid foundation on which I rebuilt my life.

~ J.K. Rowling

CHAPTER 3

PUMPING IRON

I STILL FIND it interesting, as well as strange, that exercise was suggested to me as a "by the way, this might help you too". Even within the clinic itself, the exercise program was minimal. There was a very small gym with limited equipment and it was generally empty. They also held yoga classes a few times per week for the inpatients, but that was really the extent of it.

Little did I know then that this simple beginning to "move" was going to become my core foundation for recovery and ongoing wellness.

My psychologist also suggested I should join a regular gym, and knowing that almost all of my family were members of the local Fitness First gym, I decided to join them there. This had the benefit of family encouragement and support and a bonus for them was that I was within an earshot so they could further monitor my movements.

Now, keep in mind that I was far from the fit woman I am today, but as the weeks went by, not only was my mind healing but also my body from years of neglect and abuse. Six months before I crashed, my diet had mainly consisted of Sustagen powder and alcohol. On the days I could stomach food, it would be nothing more than a strawberry smoothie or some two-minute noodles. Then, of course, the constant diarrhoea meant the minimal nutrients I had taken in were immediately flushed out.

I had a lot of work to do to regain good physical health.

I considered myself in previous times a "token" gym member. You know, those that make a New Year's resolution, join a gym, and go twice in a 12-month period. There were times when I went more regularly, but purely for some quick-fix aesthetic goal, certainly never long enough to ever feel the true benefits and always accompanied with a large dose of alcohol as my "sidekick".

So, this "doing it for real" thing was new for me. I would enter the gym with my head down and go directly up to the women's only area where I would play around with a fit ball and maybe sit on one of the machines and pretend I knew what I was doing. Not only was I completely out of my depth physically, but also my lack of confidence was not making things any easier.

I felt awkward, uncoordinated, and completely out of my comfort zone.

But I persisted. I was consistent. It became routine.

Within a few months, I had built up enough courage to walk through the entrance, acknowledge staff on the reception desk, and head to the downstairs cardio area where I was no longer "not visible", but I still felt safe. That need for security in the early stages of recovery was crucial and this was an important part of keeping my anxiety under control.

In AA, they introduce the H-A-L-T principle very early on—don't get too *hungry, angry, lonely,* or *tired.* In rehab therapy, we spoke about it as keeping "Even Steven". I was aware I needed to keep myself as emotionally stable as I could and this meant ensuring I didn't put myself in situations I wasn't ready for in all areas of my life.

ALCOHOL was still in my life in this first year after attending rehab… especially for my 40th night-out-on-the-town birthday party in April 2013. And I wasn't quite ready to not *CELEBRATE* that milestone. After all, I'd made it through that first year in recovery and had managed to make some real inroads to getting myself back on track.

I had set small goals of only allowing myself to drink every few months at an "event". Like most alcoholics, the thought of stopping altogether seems like an impossible task and, furthermore, boring.

I was genuinely hoping I could somehow be one of those social drinkers who could have the odd drink at a party, stop at two, and happily abstain for the rest of the night. Sadly, that was never going to be me. Once I downed the first one, a "firecracker" exploded in my brain and I had to have another, and another, and another.

The next day came the hangover and regrets, which brought on anxiety again. And I wasn't in any shape to attend training which, by then, I looked forward to… and needed.

And that's where things really started to change because I began to value my training and what it did for me psychologically more than I valued the brief alcohol-induced sedation.

The reward of not *drinking* was enormous.

About two months into joining the gym, David told me about personal trainer, Wayne Ryan, who had offered him a free PT session, and David suggested I might like one too. The very thought of a one-on-one PT session sent my anxiety levels through the roof. For heaven's sake, I'd only just progressed from the ladies' gym to the cross-trainer. Nevertheless, I knew that putting myself outside of my comfort zone was a good thing and, at that stage, I was already enjoying that "feel good" vibe with my own fitness workouts.

So, I contacted Wayne not knowing he was about to change my life.

He was a heavily-tattooed bearded ball-of-muscle and he didn't do anything in halves. He was a single father with four children under the age of 10 and had a checkered history of making poor lifestyle judgments.

As the story unfolded, Wayne told me he had used exercise and sport as part of his rehabilitation to keep him on the straight and narrow. And geez, he was really good at it.

His background was boxing and he demonstrated that "fight" mentality. It was always win or lose, and this soon became my mindset whenever I put myself on the line.

I started with one PT session per week and this quickly turned into two, and within three months, I was regularly training with Wayne three times a week at his home studio.

An avid CrossFit fan and participant, Wayne convinced me that this form of discipline was going to be everything I needed to get fitter and stronger. He was so damn passionate about this sport... and it both inspired and enthused me to follow the same path.

My sessions were regularly filled with snatches, pull-ups, rope whips, kettlebell swings, and pretty much every discipline except swimming, which he even managed to somehow squeeze in at times.

Wayne didn't allow any room for me to say "no" to anything he suggested. We simply did it. This is something I learned works well for me, provided it is still an educated and safe decision.

The harder it was for me physically, the better it was for me psychologically.

SOBRIETY can bring with it a "honeymoon" period where life feels quite euphoric, and I can most definitely attest to that. I would go to bed exhausted but look forward to the next day, up with the sun thinking about my training session, which was proving to be my "*Good Samaritan*".

This feeling was something I had not experienced since I was in my early 20s, like I had a million and one things to look forward to with opportunities galore.

I often said to David, "The days are not long enough", contradictory to the previous few years when I wished for the days to end quickly so I could close my eyes, sleep, and forget about things for a while.

Exercise was becoming a passion. I could not wait for the next session, and admittedly, sometimes I pushed myself a bit too hard. I'd train just for the sake of training because it provided me with a rush of natural adrenaline that was hard to beat. Those around me wondered whether I was swapping one addiction for another. But they need not have been concerned because the health benefits of this exercise recovery regime were becoming obvious.

One of the most beautiful things about this period was my family's support. David was still working away in Melbourne every fortnight and the kids were only 10 and seven, so just like every other working parent, I was juggling all my motherly responsibilities with my training.

God knows this was *not* something I wanted to stuff up.

My parents would often look after Evie and Wilson, Cassie was always making herself available, and even my 80-something-year-old at the time nana (Irene) would have them over in the evenings, feed them, and watch television with them until I finished at the gym. When David was home, we would "tag-team" with our parental responsibilities or train together whenever we could.

It was so uplifting to have the full support of family to pursue this integral part of getting my life back in order.

All recoveries from addictions are different, but for me, I required distractions... the distraction from my old behaviour and lifestyle, and most of all, a distraction from my anxious thoughts.

After a few months, I found weekdays easier to manage with my work as a corporate trainer, the children and their schooling, and general parenting. During the week, there was little time for contemplation and a busy schedule that provided me with a 'constant'.

But the casual weekends and social occasions were triggering some fidgeting and persistent restlessness. To avoid my Friday evenings becoming knee-deep in wine, which was my previous default, I took the kids on beachside walks with their scooters and we enjoyed the Gold Coast sunsets together. The water, the sand, and that evening sky were everything someone searching for internal peace could ever wish for. The connection between Mother Nature and my soul was bringing me an underlying comfort and reassurance.

Remarkably, after 30 minutes of this kind of ritual, I was calm, relaxed, and not wanting to pick up a drink. It was working.

Wayne and I began monitoring my lifts and fitness levels and seeing the progress on paper was exciting and empowering. When I completed my first CrossFit WOD, although thoroughly exhausted, I had tears of joy *streaming* down my face. I was caught off-guard.

The enormity of what I had achieved in such a short period both took my breath away and hugged my heart at the exact same time. Six months earlier, I could not have done that.

I felt so powerful.

This sport, this discipline, and this relentless pursuit to push my body to the limits had transcended to feeling psychologically strong. I was back in full control.

The Crossfit Box where I began to learn the correlation between physical and mental strength.

My evening walks on the beach distracted me from thinking about alcohol and broke the 'itchy feet' feelings.

One of the many scooter rides with the kids along the
esplanade.

One of the first images where my eyes were clear and my
head was beginning to follow.

My Sobriety Step 3

- Start exercising DAILY.
- SCHEDULE this into your routine.
- Remember exercise can be as little as a 30-minute walk outside.
- Find a friend or family member to start working out with.
- Join a gym or program where health is everyone's focus.
- Hire a personal trainer to make you accountable.

All you need is 20 seconds of insane courage and I promise you something great will come of it.

~ Benjamin Mee
~ We bought a Zoo

CHAPTER 4

WEIGHT ON MY MIND

FOR A NUMBER of years before reaching out for help, my nutrition was nothing short of appalling. By crunch time in January 2012, my weight had plummeted to a mere 47kg. I was just skin and bone. Healthy eating was not part of my diet. The alcohol was providing me with my entrée, main, and dessert.

With Evie being diagnosed with type 1 diabetes in 2009, I quickly became au fait with the importance of a balanced diet, counting carbs, and reading nutritional panels on food packets. This was just a way of life when it came to Evie and gauging correct dosages for her insulin and overall management of her diabetes. I also made sure the rest of the family ate wholesome foods, but regularly neglected myself.

A few years before my "crash", I was overweight, bloated, and sporting that "pink flushed" alcoholic face. I didn't weigh myself but I believe I hit the 70kg mark, and for someone who is 167cm tall with a slight frame, I looked and felt terrible.

In the early stages of my addiction, I was extremely lax about food choices. Often, this was the result of an alcohol binge the night before, much like that 'morning after feeling' from my younger partying days. Inevitably, the following day would always require a hangover "fix" of greasy and unhealthy food, large portions, and even larger amounts of carbs and fats.

Needless to say, the buckets of wine I was consuming on a daily basis were also a big contributor to the additional calories and subsequent weight gain. The more this went on, the more I didn't rate eating all that important. It reached a stage when it became physically difficult to consume food.

The first part of my day, I was crippled with nausea and stomach pains. I had constant diarrhoea for about a year. This became so much of an issue that I had to pre-plan my work commutes to follow a route where I could gain easy access to public toilets. And there were a number of times I didn't actually make it. I'd even become accustomed to packing an extra pair of undies in my handbag, *'just in case'*.

Memories that still haunt me.

Those days began with a cup of tea around mid-morning, and by lunchtime, the meds (Xanax or Valium) had started working with my nausea and cramps reducing. It was about then I began entertaining the thought of food—fatty, greasy stuff. By mid-afternoon, I would snack on something sweet and before you knew it, it is was "wine time" again.

By mid-2011, things worsened. The importance of being able to stomach alcohol far outweighed the need to eat.

For dinner, well, I'd eat anything I damn well wanted to because, by that time, I simply didn't care.

And by December that same year, I had dramatically dropped 15kg. Family and friends were now beginning to witness that something was going horribly wrong.

My doctor became highly concerned with my frequent visits. I was sick all the time—colds, gastro, and even a serious bronchial infection that wouldn't shift. I was constantly bed-ridden either from illness, a hangover, or knocked out cold from booze.

My faculties were kaput. I even woke up one morning in agony with my left hand severely broken in three places. I had no recollection of how this happened. My theory was that I had gotten up in the middle of the night to go to the bathroom and fallen into a wall or on the floor, but nothing I could even remotely remember. This was a very interesting conversation with my doctor that entailed a number of white lies.

The fractures took months to heal due to my body being in such poor health.

At this point, I knew I was in trouble and deep down I wanted to help myself, but I was so far gone, I didn't know what to do.

I really couldn't see a way out.

At the suggestion of my GP, I became a regular consumer of Sustagen powder. With my first purchase, I gave the pharmacist a convoluted reason as to why I couldn't just eat food.

The little white lies continued... it became a survival technique. My body was so acidic and toxic that food made me gag and vomit. Yet, this proven formula of nutrient-packed meal replacements, usually for oldies, probably kept me alive. I am sure of it.

In November 2011, my mum had flown down from Queensland to help me pack up my house. The severity of my weight loss had frightened the life out of her. She would plead with me to eat and I tried... I really tried. I was also not the nicest person to be around at this time. I was angry and defensive and I would argue that I just couldn't stomach nutritious food. And even in my haze of numbness, I could still see her face of desperation. The only thing I could hold down was a McDonald's strawberry smoothie and she took that as an opportunity to provide me with some fuel.

The starvation and alcohol-only diet continued until I went to rehab. My body was desperately in need of repair. My rehab support team made it a priority to just get me *eating*. Eating anything! The daily buffet at the clinic was a good calorie booster and, within a month, I gained 5kg.

My new GP on the Gold Coast was now regularly testing my bloods, and by all accounts, everything was improving.

Particularly with my liver function, nutrient absorption, and previously alarmingly high triglycerides. Things were moving in the right direction.

Healthy eating balanced out my gut health and I automatically felt less anxious. What I put in my mouth affected me both physically and psychologically. Brain food was now on the menu with salmon, nuts, avocados, fruits, eggs, etc. This nourishment started regulating my hormones and stabilising my moods along with the important weight gain. And although I was training six days a week, the calories *in* versus calories *out* were not evening out.

The progression through recovery made me realise there is a tipping point for me with most things in life. From work to home life, to relationships, and everything else in between, I constantly walk a fine line psychologically with what I can and can't deal with. That includes feeling uncomfortable aesthetically, which will have a further impact on my mental state. When my pants begin to feel tight, literally, my anxiety rises. This is how I feel when I gain weight, particularly around my waist. And in a world where there are myriad things I can't control, this is one I feel I can.

The fitness journey with my tattooed trainer, Wayne, sparked my curiosity about what else I could do to further enhance this "happy" feeling.

So, I enlisted the help of a nutrition coach to assist in gaining better control of my caloric intake and educate me about counting macronutrients. And so began my love affair, "flexible dieting", which allowed me to maintain the best body composition I have ever had without feeling restricted in my choice of foods.

With OCD still being with me today, the importance of being the one in control of my diet without having to adhere to someone else's meal plan is absolute key. The knowledge I gained from flexible dieting gave me an insight into what my body *and* brain liked.

I began to track my intake and was guided towards the amounts of protein, fats, and carbohydrates I needed to develop lean muscle mass and slowly reduce body fat, while undertaking a structured weight training program. Within weeks, there were significant physical changes and, more importantly, my mind loved me calling the shots with what I chose to put in my mouth.

Strict adherence to dietary protocols meant my body was responding aesthetically. The effort I had been putting in was beginning to show results. This combination of eating nutrient-dense foods that both my brain and body loved whilst still ensuring these values didn't make me gain additional weight, feel deflated, and unbalanced was working.

I was onto another winner.

My meal prep was full of good nutritious food, but also for the first time calories controlled.

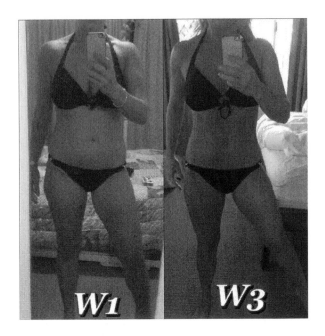

Within 3 weeks of adhering to these new protocols, my body was responding.

Sandi Louise Ross

Bhsc Naturopath & Acupuncture

Masters Chinese Medicine

To make healthy mood hormones known as neurotransmitters, the body requires specific nutrients to be consumed via the diet and absorbed. The common happy brain hormones are serotonin and dopamine and up to 90% of serotonin is produced in the gut! The vicious cycle with addiction, particularly alcohol is that all types of alcohol are detrimental to our beneficial gut bacteria, and lead to an out of balance ecology.

The body is very good at utilizing the minimal nutrition given to the body, that's how we survive, but it doesn't mean we thrive. When we are not eating the right macro-nutrients, we are running low on resources to make feel-good hormones. By providing good quality protein, the body receives building blocks required to make our happy mood hormones. In addition, we need good digestion to break down the protein into the small particles the body can absorb. Stress in particular inhibits absorption as it diverts blood away from digestion to our muscles to "fight or flight". Furthermore, micronutrients known as co-factors are like the glue and nails to the building blocks, and without these, we cannot convert the proteins into the happy mood hormones. Micronutrients are found in wholefoods particularly plants.

By having an output for stress via exercise, then providing good macro and micronutrients, Justine was able to make happy mood hormones once again, helping empower her further.

My Sobriety Step 4

- Have a full blood work-up done to establish any deficiencies.

- Start nourishing your body with good nutritious foods.

- Eat regular meals and don't allow yourself to get too hungry.

- Drink at least two litres of water per day.

- If needed, take supplementation to give your body an extra boost.

- Keep junk food and overly processed food at a minimum.

- Enlist the help of a nutritionist if you are still unsure.

We must all choose between what is right and what is easy.

~ Albus Dumbledore

CHAPTER 5

LETTING GO OF FEAR

MY **CONFIDENCE** was building towards the end of 2012 with my fitness abilities. I was learning how putting myself outside of my comfort zone was benefiting me psychologically and my head was in a much better place after a year of step-by-step effort.

For the first time since my 20s, I was beginning to feel like I wanted to do more and that I was capable of achieving something outside of what I knew.

I had a passion for living a full and exciting life again.

David, Evie, and Wilson encouraged me to enter the January 13 Robina Mini-Triathlon called *The Enticer*. It was a 300m open lake swim, 8km cycle, and a 2.5km run. Was I up for it? Yes, but self-doubt was definitely present.

Wayne helped me set up a training program to cover all disciplines. In the months leading up to the event, I struggled to get my head around what I had set myself. I would like to think the name of the race itself would be enough to keep me excited in those months leading up to the event, but I struggled on a daily basis to get my head around what I'd just committed to. Negative thoughts and self-sabotaging statements were slowly making me come undone and I questioned my ability to achieve this goal.

"*What if I get pushed under in the water? What if I can't breathe? What happens if I can't find my bike? What happens if my feet slip off the pedals? What happens if I can't run the distance and have to walk? What will people think if they see me walking? What if I come last?*" And the best one of all: "*What if I am so tired at my 4.30 am rise on the day that I fall asleep in the race?*"

Knowing what I do now about Obsessive Compulsive Disorder, I am aware that one of my major triggers is stress and overwhelm. It was bound to happen. Oh my God, I literally made myself sick with these relentless thoughts.

Yet, I knew I must keep moving forward. My desire to conquer my anxiety for the first time in years was overriding the ruminating thoughts. I got up every day and followed my plan, ate the right foods, and focused on going through the motions. By this time, I was well and truly in a routine of eat, train, and sleep so this was just an extension of that format.

One thing that gave me a big boost of confidence came from Evie on one of my training runs around the suburban block when she was riding her bike beside me. This was something that she had started doing from day one of my preparation for the race. Running was my least favourite of the legs and I was struggling to keep momentum and the hurt was kicking in.

When I said to my little girl, who was only 10, I didn't think I could do it, she said: "Mum, pain is just weakness leaving your body. You can do this".

In that moment, something in me snapped and I managed to find the courage to push through the pain and push on.

On the eve of the race, I went to the course to complete my final registration and rack my bike in the enclosure. I had hoped that becoming more familiar with what the track was going to look like would somehow make me feel calmer. In some ways, it did. At least I knew where my bike was and where each leg started and ended. That feeling of being prepared gave me a little more comfort, but on the other hand, it fuelled my anxiety further as I had a visual of what I was in for. But damned if you do, damned if you don't.

I had intended on going to bed really early and getting as much sleep as possible to ensure I had the energy to "smash it". But true to form, my mind had another agenda and this was not going to be the case.

I had my race gear packed and I'd checked it over and over and then over and over again. David stepped in to help rid me of this manic episode. He took me to my bag, went through each item on the checklist, marked it off, and together, we agreed it was all there.

It always amazes me how the mind has the ability to doubt its own judgments, but when someone else verifies what you already know to be true, amazingly, it becomes an opinion you trust. Anyhow, it worked. I went to bed, fell asleep, and woke with my 4.30 alarm.

Driving to the race venue, I think I hyperventilated twice, not to mention the numerous trips to the toilet before we left. We arrived; I got my tri-suit on, and then made another quick dash to the porta loos. I anxiously waited for the call to move to the starting line with David and the kids got themselves a prime position to see my first leg. My parents had also come along for support and were already settled in.

I felt physically ill as I lined up in my over-40s age category with about 30 other women. The swim was first and although it was my strongest leg in pool training, the lake looked like the English Channel and my confidence began to sink.

My heart was racing so fast, I felt like I was going to pass out. In came the negative thoughts again: *"What if I can't get to the other side? What if someone pushes me under? What if I have to get pulled out of the water?"*

Can't turn back now. Crack went the starter's gun and I dived into the water. Limbs thrashing about everywhere as everyone was jostling for positions. There were legs in my face, water going up my nose, and I thought I was going to drown. My pre-race plan went down the gurgler and I thought I could not continue, even having to call the officials to pull me out. The panic was real.

But somewhere in the murky mayhem, I mustered up the will to keep going; to let go of fear. My immediate thought was to reach the other side. I ditched the freestyle, stuck my head above the water, and dog-paddled across the lake. When my feet touched the shore, I hit the ground running. I had done it.

David, the kids, and my mum and "dad" were there waiting near the bike changeover. Even though I was dragging the chain, they still clapped and waved to me as I ran to my bike. Seeing their encouraging faces was just the thing I needed to keep me going.

The transition was fairly smooth and my legs were ticking over on the pedals. It felt great. The wind was against us but I felt strong. That 8km seemed to go fairly quickly, and even though I was hurting a little, it wasn't enough to slow me down. I clocked a faster time than at training.

The run was my weakest leg but I maintained a steady pace for the first 1km. Even though I promised myself I wouldn't walk, I had to. The gruelling effort forced me to stop twice to catch my breath. But I was determined not to throw the towel in.

Approaching the finish line, I had this amazing burst of energy and I picked up the pace. There were crowds of people cheering their loved ones on and my eyes welled up when I saw mine.

I pushed as hard as I could and ran through the finishing arches. I did it, I bloody did it… and what a relief. I felt so proud that I had come so far from the clutches of alcoholic hell to achieve such an important personal "victory".

This was so much more than physical. I had pushed myself psychologically harder than I could ever remember and found an inner strength I never knew I had.

The tally that day was:

Me: 1. Anxiety and self-doubt: 0.

Crossing that finish line was one of the greatest moments
of my life.

My head was playing all sorts of tricks on me here.

Finally reaching the end of the swim leg.

My Sobriety Step 5

- Set yourself a challenge with your exercise.
- Choose something that requires you to be consistent.
- Focus as much of your time as you can on your health (less time to focus on alcohol).
- Announce your goal to others to make you accountable.
- Create a plan that ensures you achieve this.
- Structure a schedule that makes this a priority.
- If required, register for the event early.

Don't you dare give up!

CHAPTER 6

RAISING THE BAR

STEPPING into the world of sobriety meant I was stepping out of a shattered-mind, time-wasting former life into a clear-headed new dawning where I was constantly looking for worthwhile things to do and ways to fill up my days. Yet, I still had my moments.

Occasionally, I found myself needing to fill up those silent moments when my head began playing tricks on me.

I read somewhere about the importance of being "still" and "alone" with one's thoughts, but that never really worked for me. Too much alone time gave me the opportunity to dwell on "monstrosities" I created under the influence and, gosh, was that a huge mind game I did not enjoy.

Reliving times when you are at your worst is one of the easiest ways to tip you backwards… and the associated guilt is enough to send you right back to "medicating".

Self-pity can have the exact same effect. The old "*poor me, pour me another drink*" expression is something to be avoided when on the road to recovery.

Although I did not follow an AA program, I did take note of the *Twelve Steps'* guidelines, and the following were important to me:

Step 4: Made a searching and fearless moral inventory of ourselves.

Step 5: Admitted to God, to ourselves, and to another human being the exact nature of our wrongs.

These two steps were a necessary part of any recovery process, regardless of whether you believe in God or not. Ultimately, it's about taking responsibility without torturing yourself to the point where you drink again. That is why the next two steps are also crucial to undertake:

Step 6: Were entirely ready to have God remove all these defects of character.

Step 7: Humbly asked Him to remove our shortcomings.

For me, one of the most valuable distractions from negative thoughts was my focus on self-improvement. The longer I worked at it, the greater the momentum. It reached the stage where I started to enjoy going to the gym. It was my base camp for becoming physically fit and generally healthy. After my brain and body had been put through the wringer for so many years, I loved how training with weights made me feel mentally as well as aesthetically.

My coach in 2014 was Nick Cheadle, and in May, I told him I wanted to enter my first Musclemania Ms Bikini Australia championships later that year at the Chandler Sports Centre in Brisbane. I was 41, and one half of me was saying "Are you seriously crazy?" while the other half said, "Just do it".

Fuelling my desire was when David said, "Babe, you're not 21 anymore," when he saw me admiring a pair of short-shorts a younger woman was wearing at a shopping centre. That went down like a ton of bricks and stoked my determination to enter… and I signed up.

Nick was based in Sydney, so all of our preparatory communicating was online. He set out a program of training and nutritional intake. Body sculpting was paramount and this meant hitting the weights in the "big boys" area of the gym. Morning sessions were cardio on the treadmill and evenings were all about building lean muscle mass. I was absorbing it all with a passion.

I started my prep at around 59kg, and by the time I went on stage in September, I was 53kg. David and the kids were there in support and the pre-competition anxiety was much the same as in the mini-triathlon a year earlier.

Backstage, I was very nervous, and seeing the other girls, I knew I was not even in the game. They were sub 10% body fat and I was around 15%. Nick and I knew we had not left enough time to build the lean muscle tone to be competitive. Nevertheless, I gave it my best shot.

I did not receive a call out for any placings, which I had hoped for. It was a body blow. And to make matters worse, Evie, who was 12, ran up to me and started sobbing, saying: "Mum, I just really, really wanted you to win because you have worked so hard". What a powerful moment in time. This was the point where I realized the impact my pursuits had on my children. They were watching their mum go out on a limb and work hard to achieve a goal she had set.

What I reminded her of at that point (and myself) was that it did not matter that I did not win.

> *What mattered was I set myself a goal to get myself on stage and I committed to that in every way. This was more than enough.*

Later, I had a thirst to finish what I had started, and properly next time.

Fitness modelling competitions are not top of my list, but at that time, the training and preparation routine suited me to a tee. I needed that structure.

My OCD was catered for as life was very much regimented and controlled in the lead-up to the 2015 competition. Meals were organised and my training schedule set in stone. My mindset and self-discipline were my daily life.

One day, I was in the gym and had only completed two of the three sets of leg extensions and was fatiguing. I picked up my gym bag and headed for the car. But my head was not going to allow that, so I went back and completed the workout.

Since cutting alcohol out of my life and taking on rigorous fitness programs, I had not had a single cold or flu.

Come September and I was ready this time for the Musclemania Ms Bikini Australia Division 35-plus. The adrenaline and nerves kicked in again and calming mantras I had been chanting were replaced with panic. I remember saying, "Breathe, Justine, and just keep bloody breathing".

My category was ushered to the side entrance and, one by one, our names were called to the stage. I don't know where it came from but, suddenly, the mania dropped and I strutted on stage like a proud peacock. Maybe it was the music that prodded me along but the feeling was reminiscent of my days in the music industry. That place on stage where I could be lost in the moment and almost in a character-like state. As strange as this sounds, this for me was a 'safe' feeling.

When it came to the judges' announcements, my name was called in third place. That felt *soooo* good. Standing on stage hearing my name called in one of the top positions was so surreal. To think that only three years earlier I was suffocating in my own despair, dying from the inside out, and living in my own private and sometimes public hell.

Once again, I had beaten that ruinous voice in my head that continually told me I couldn't and I wouldn't.

My first competition in 2014 where I did not place but
learnt the power of commitment.

Placing 3rd in my category at Musclemania 2015.

The Jungle Jane themewear round.

With my biggest supporter David there to cheer me on.

Once again I had beaten those persistent voices in my
head that kept telling me I couldn't.

My Sobriety Step 6

- Remember to congratulate yourself for achieving success.
- Constantly re-evaluate your goals.
- Once you have completed one, move on to the next, even if small.
- Just because you didn't achieve your goal doesn't mean you won't ever again.
- Do the work and put in the time.
- Keep the structure and schedule that keeps you on track.
- Idle time often ends you back up into bad habits.

I am worth it.

CHAPTER 7

GOING TO 'CHURCH'

THE GYM was where I started to feel I fitted in. I was part of a community of people who gathered in their "church" to, in many cases, regain control of their lives and rebuild their strength in a metaphoric sense. And we all had a story.

The gym was a place I felt safe. I trained on Friday and Saturday nights and learned that the attendees those evenings were there for different reasons, including competing in bodybuilding or fitness competitions; thrived on the routine and what it did for their mental health; to avoid putting themselves in harm's way; escaping negative people; just on their own.

While the "rest of the world" was celebrating the end of the week with a few rounds of drinks with work mates or friends, that kind of bar was not an option for me. I was choosing the 'iron' option.

At the gym, I progressively made friends chatting in the breaks and it was interesting the stories they told, stories that did not go outside the building. These connections and their anecdotes gave me comfort in knowing I was not alone; I was understood.

When you are in recovery, surrounding yourself with like-minded people is important. That doesn't just mean "fit and healthy" people. It means people who understand your position on sobriety, people who take into consideration what is best for you, what you are exposed to, and the type of activity and environment they involve you in.

It can be extremely confronting when you realise that a great deal of your connection with people is underpinned by drinking. Finding another form of commonality can be hard.

In my own coaching business today, I am blown away by the number of clients who confide in me that they are often pressured to drink by family and friends. When they have made the extremely difficult decision to cut down or even cut out alcohol, they are ridiculed and harassed with unhelpful comments such as:

"What do you mean you're not drinking this Christmas!?

Surely this is just a phase you are going through!

I'm going to have to find another friend!

You are way more fun when you drink!

Do you really mean not EVER again?"

Disappointingly, many of these disparaging remarks come from parents and family members.

One client attending a family barbecue was ridiculed about why she wasn't having a drink and why it was she couldn't just have one. She silenced her critics when she screamed at the top of her lungs: "Because I hate who I am when I drink!"

Another client told her mother she would not be drinking when she visited on holidays, to which her mother replied, "Well, that is just ridiculous".

These are situations that can cause a great deal of torment and trauma for an addict who is doing his or her best to get "clean". Hurtful words can cause an addict to slide back into the whirlpool of swill. It makes my blood boil when I hear this.

When I first became sober, like many addicts, I believed I would still be able to attend social events where the booze was flowing freely… and not be tempted.

I felt I should be strong enough to resist… yet another unrealistic expectation I had set for myself.

Rehab counsellors told us it is vitally important to embrace "self-protect" mode; to stay away from social gatherings where you could be tempted to down one or two or more.

With this in mind, I started to pick and choose the people I caught up with and even a "safe" time of day we met. For example, a breakfast was always going to be less risky than a dinner when wine would be on offer.

Over time, I became more and more confident in my ability to say "no" and people stopped asking if I would like a drink. They knew that having a drink was not part of the catch-up for me.

I couldn't have been more blessed with how David responded to my dramatic transformation. I really did get lucky with him, even though he pushed the limits for a number of years. Alcohol had been an involved part of the way we interacted as a couple. With it gone, there was a lot of clearing up of old messes. Alcohol had affected my ability to express what I was feeling and what I needed in our marriage. It required a lot of work to rebuild what had been lost.

When I finished my stint at the clinic, it was his decision to no longer drink at home, unless we had people over for a special occasion. David cut back his consumption dramatically. If we were out socially and I felt uncomfortable, he was all over it. The minute I felt vulnerable, he was protecting me. He still does. When I am ready to go home, he calls it the "exit strategy". This kind of support is what every recovering addict needs and deserves.

And with my new-found love for training, David also pushed himself into fitness and we joined forces. Weekends became much more about physical activity as a family. Bike rides, long walks along the beach, gym sessions, and genuinely enjoying the moment.

I also felt my children would benefit from doing more exercise. We were no longer in Melbourne where we were so often indoors due to poor weather. Sunshine and blue skies were now in abundance. I was also keen for them to have something I hadn't had early in life—a healthy outlet they could turn to as a way of strengthening bodies and minds so they would be able to deal with life's challenges. For every mistake I made and hurt from, I prayed they never have to experience any of it.

The adage *"birds of a feather flock together"* is definitely the case for both sides of the wellness spectrum. People who have an issue with alcohol tend to have an issue with someone who doesn't drink. It simply highlights their own problem. When you are taking part in an activity that is accepted within a group, this can be seen as normal behaviour, even if it's harmful. It's also difficult to have true perspective in these situations and even more so, change.

It's interesting to observe people and their relationship with alcohol. I have likened myself to a sniffer dog when it comes to identifying problem-drinkers. Many disguise their alcoholism with justifications for attending event after event after event. In fact, the opening of an envelope would seem like an acceptable reason to pop the champagne. While I am wanting to keep these people at arm's length, I find myself also wanting to save them from their misery.

For my own protection, it is not wise for me to spend too much time with people who regularly imbibe. It always will be a reminder of the grasp alcohol had on me and how desperate I once was to drink. When the opportunity presents itself, I use the story of my own recovery as an example of "what can be" for those caught in the trap.

Today, my social circle is relatively small, yet not restricted. Like most of us who have children, busy workloads, and full lives, social events tend to be few and far between.

My family and friends are so incredibly supportive of the need for me to keep my mental and physical health at an optimum. I am still checked up on regularly by those who are close to me. This would not be the case if I had not acknowledged I needed help and gone through a lifestyle overhaul, which included eliminating people and environments that no longer served me.

Weekends are always spent doing something active.

The gym is where I found so many like minded people.

This lifestyle has allowed David to have his very own transformation.

Our weekends are full of healthy living adventures.

My Sobriety Step 7

- Establish which friends endorse your sober life.
- Don't be afraid to let some people go that hinder your recovery.
- Socialise at times that allow you the greatest chance of being sober.
- Do not be afraid to say no to an invitation if you are not ready.
- Have a sober safe plan for socializing.
- Join a group or club that encourages a healthy lifestyle.

The first step to getting anywhere is to decide you're no longer willing to stay where you are.

~ Author unknown.

CHAPTER 8

THE MAINTENANCE

I'T'S A SAD FACT that recovered alcoholics can so easily give in to temptation and fall off the sober wagon. To make massive lifestyle changes is one thing, but to remain sober when that quest for change dwindles is another.

When I first went into rehab, it was apparent it was a matter of life or death. Implementation of all the necessary strategies was clear, concise, and well-constructed.

After I got a handle on some of the most important matters, like not drinking, there was a calmness that could have given me a false sense of security that everything was now fixed. It wasn't.

The first year, I thought and hoped I could be a social drinker. Rarely does someone go into rehab for the first time truly thinking they are going to have to give up their "crutch" forever, especially when it comes to alcohol.

The thought of entering the social arena without a drink in hand *ever* was not something I could grasp early on. I mean, where would I find the courage to be confident and, more importantly, how would I even have fun if I didn't drink?

So, I picked a few special occasions where I would allow myself to drink, but set myself limits. After a few failed attempts, I realised social drinking was not going to work because I could never stop at one.

After that first glass, the calling for more overrode my brain telling me "that's enough". I would try so hard to stick to my plan, but it never worked. I continually disappointed myself.

The next morning, I felt like shit. Anxiety would be back with a vengeance, and to make the situation even worse, my much-loved training would take a back seat for the next 48 hours. There was no way a nauseated and fragile version of me could build up the energy and strength for a workout. That didn't sit well with me because my fitness was what was keeping me on track.

Arrive 2013 and there were three unmemorable occasions I let my guard down. The first was my 40th birthday party in April as previously mentioned, when the champagne flowed at a Broadbeach nightclub venue. For most of the night, my drinking felt social... until about the third champagne in.

The second occasion was my Personal Training course graduation in August, and the third was a work Christmas party on December 13th.

Despite setting myself drinking limits and my family watching me like a hawk, I just couldn't stop. I downed the ones they could see and then moved on to the hidden ones. A familiar activity and one I secretly despised.

At the Christmas party, I promised myself I would not drink at the restaurant dinner, only afterwards at the Broadbeach nightclub we all went to. I was hoping this would help "minimise the damage".

When we arrived at the club, I was handed a glass of champagne. It went down like lolly water and that warm, fuzzy feeling swept over me quickly. After all, it had been four months since my last drink.

Then came the second, third, and fourth in fairly quick succession, with chasers to follow.

We moved on to another club and I was confronted with entrance stairs "the size of Mt Everest". It didn't help that I was wearing new platform shoes with six-inch heels, not to mention my state of inebriation.

Attempting the flight ended badly when I lost my footing and fell backwards down the stairs. A burly security guard asked me to leave and I hurled abuse at him for "incorrectly" assessing my condition as drunk. He was right, of course.

A friend assisted me to a cab.

Arriving home, I passed out. The morning-after effects were "deadly". Shaking, heart palpitations, a racing mind, and awful nausea. In the old days, this would be when I would start topping up or taking medication to come down. But this time, I just rode it out… painfully.

I drove my sore and sorry backside to Macca's drive-through, bought a cheeseburger and large lemonade, and sat up at my favourite beachside lookout on Burleigh Hill trying to recall how and why this had happened again.

I decided there and then that this 'social' drinking just does not work for me anymore. I didn't have a "better" time drinking, I didn't "feel" wonderful, and I just never wanted to feel that way ever again.

And that was my last drink.

This image was taken before I went out on the 13th December 2013, the date that later would become my 'sober anniversary'.

Alcohol is the most accepted, promoted, condoned, and expected drug of choice on Earth. It is the only drug you will have to justify why you are "not" taking it.

Our culture is built around socializing with alcohol, celebrating with alcohol, relaxing with alcohol and, in myriad cases, medicating with alcohol.

When your best friend calls you in deep distress because she has just broken up with her boyfriend, after initially consoling her with all of the usual "men are shit" comments, she is then invited over to your house to drown her sorrows with a bottle of champagne. Because that is what fixes everything, right?

This kind of "what are friends for" sympathetic comforting is what magnifies dependency on alcohol and leaves no room for natural and long-term alternatives for dealing with stress and trauma.

When I was in group therapy at the clinic, an activity we undertook was to set up a wellness or safety plan. This included ways to reduce our stress and temptation to re-abuse by managing how and when we socialised.

My plan included initially catching up with friends for breakfast, rather than lunch or dinner. That way I knew wine would not be on the menu for brekkie.

I structured my days so there would be very little to overwhelm me and my evenings were spent being distracted by television and children. And in the "witching" hours between 4 pm and 7 pm, that packing up of the kids and their scooters and walking the beachfront had already proved to be a winner. There were also other times where I would drop into family unannounced just to pass the time. This too was a lifesaver.

Before I knew it, the kind of risky social situations I dreaded were becoming less scary. The thought of having a drink became less and less important until, one day, I realised I had not thought about it for weeks.

With David deciding not to drink at home—to the point where he was almost a non-drinker—my life was so much easier.

As a fitness and life coach, I have worked with many women who are trying to get their lives back on track, but their husbands/partners are just not on board. They see the problem as not theirs and, therefore, restricting alcohol at home is not an option.

I have also known about the sabotage that led to emotional abuse from their partners and these wonderful women have succumbed again to drinking because it was far too difficult to continue with the recovery process. Their plight had literally been sabotaged.

I feel deep empathy for those who are on a path of recovery but don't have the kind of support I had.

Your home life will make or break you.

When David was away travelling with work, my family would do everything they could to ensure I got to the gym, including last-minute drop-offs with the kids. Everyone who was close to me saw how fitness was an integral part of my sobriety and would do everything they could to ensure I got my training fix.

Getting adequate sleep is a must. In fact, I could possibly have dedicated an entire chapter to this. There are so many benefits to good quality sleep apart from the fact that it refreshes and energizes you.

What happens to the brain when you are asleep is astounding, and when this is compromised, you are open to exacerbating pre-existing mental health conditions and potentially creating new ones.

They say, "You can't argue with a tired brain," and when anxiety creeps in, that factor alone can make it feel so much worse. In the early days of recovery, falling asleep was an issue. I'd become so accustomed to years of being 'sleepy' by the time I got into bed. Then I was faced with the polar opposite. I'd lay awake staring at the ceiling and pray I would fall asleep as fast as possible. This was the time where I would go over and over my 'failings' of the past few years and further raise my anxiety levels, in turn, making it harder and harder to fall asleep.

It was actually like a form of torture.

But with intense training, my body naturally became tired in the evenings and, with the help of natural herbal anxiety medication, I was able to fall asleep more easily, thoughts were less dominating, and I could eliminate those ruminating pictures inside my head.

Having a solid daily routine will greatly assist recovery. And that should include some real "non-negotiables"— regular body movement, good nutrition, adequate sleep, and time for self-care activities. These are such basic human needs for survival, yet we often put them on our least important list.

And just because you have put that drink down does not mean you can stop the recovery process that helped you get sober.

For an addict or someone who is simply trying to get on top of mental health issues, these steps are imperative to long-term wellness.

My Sobriety Step 8

- Continue to keep yourself occupied with new activities.
- Do not ever become complacent.
- Alcohol may be absent but the alcoholic 'thinking' may still be there.
- Keep focused on that healthy lifestyle long-term.
- Find a way to manage your stress daily.
- Continue to get good quality sleep.

Sometimes the wrong choices

bring us to the right places.

CHAPTER 9

RUNNING ON EMPTY

MY **TRANSFORMED** lifestyle was so set in stone that became my "new normal". Consciously, I was living this "new me" every day, but subconsciously, I did not realise the enormity of the achievements I had made.

I became somewhat nonchalant about my new-found happiness that I took it for granted that I had worked so hard to get there. At times, it felt like I was simply going through the motions.

I have been reluctant to give myself credit for the effort I put in to get sober; to be kind to myself and forgive myself for being human; to love myself unconditionally and remember that I don't have to have my shit together all of the time.

Since 2012, I have had two major breakdowns, the most recent in 2019. After a volatile end to 2018 with some very serious personal family issues, I found myself pushed to the edge with stress. My cortisol had been high for weeks and I knew that what was going on in our lives was affecting me physically.

Time to fill you in on another major change to my life.

In 2016, through some routine blood tests, it was discovered that I too had diabetes. At that initial point, there was some 'to-ing and fro-ing' from a type 2 to type 1 and something in between diagnosis. To be honest, I tried to shut this out and did everything I could naturally to keep my blood sugar levels stable and, most of the time, they were.

However, in 2017, after some further testing, it was determined I was positive for GAD65 antibodies, which according to diabetes.co.uk amongst other medical research articles, are present in approximately 75% of type 1 diabetics. At that point, I was still definitely in what is known as the 'honeymoon' period and I could potentially get away with oral medication for a short time.

So, after a seriously stressful few months prior, in February 2019, my endocrinologist told me my type 1 diabetes "honeymoon" was over and I had to begin insulin treatment full-time. Even though I knew in the back of my head this was always going to eventuate, I was psychologically unprepared for it.

I had spent the past 10 years preaching to my daughter (diagnosed at seven) that type 1 diabetes was not a disability and that it would not affect her doing or being anything she wanted to be.

Now the shoe was on the other foot and I had trouble accepting my own advice.

I saw this as a "life sentence" and panicked about what these new changes were going to mean in both the short and long-term.

In retrospect, what I didn't do was allow myself to grieve. I felt I didn't have a right to do so, considering Evie had spent most of her short life with this disease and I was lucky enough to escape the first 45 of mine.

To take my mind off this life-changing news, I took on more work. My online client base grew through the roof and I was working non-stop helping others to get control of their lives… to the detriment of my own.

A month later, I went on what turned out to be a "recharge" break with David to Bali for our 10th wedding anniversary. I was already running on empty and my immune system was clearly low.

What I didn't count on was catching Bali Belly, which I took months to recover from. On top of that, I was having an adverse reaction to a prescribed medication and was unaware of it for at least a month.

Come April, I crashed. My adrenals and nervous system were so under the pump that I experienced 24/7 panic attacks and delusional-like thoughts and obsessive-compulsive behaviour. I was so unwell, I lost 5kg within weeks and dropped to under 50kg for the first time since being in recovery.

Amid all of this mania, I was also having PTSD (post-traumatic stress disorder) symptoms and reliving a lot of my past, which I thought I had put to bed. I was waking six to seven times each night, adrenaline-fuelled, barely ate, spent half the morning in the toilet with diarrhoea, and started to become agoraphobic. The thought of entering a supermarket terrified me.

I had not felt this level of anxiety since I was drinking and the overthinking was relentless. "*Would I recover? Would I ever feel normal again? How was I going to shut my brain off?*" And the biggest question, *"Am I relapsing?"*

In the past, I drank my way through it, but this was no longer an option. But to my own credit, not once did I feel the need to drink. Yet I had no idea how I was going to rid myself of this psychological overwhelm.

I worked with my naturopath and GP, and together, they decided I needed to circuit-break the nervous system with a small amount of medication for a short period of time.

I bucked against this idea. My self-talk was ridiculous… and LOUD: "*What a failure you are to not be in control of your thoughts! If you take the medication, you will rely on it forever. You should be able to do this naturally. What a shit mum you are for having to take medication to function.*"

The only thing that changes with sobriety is that you are dealing with everything that was there before in a non-anaesthetised state. You are acutely aware that if you don't start changing the way you think or reframe the past, you are headed back into waters that will swallow you up and spit you out.

I had spent 40-plus years with an extremely harsh "inner critic" as my closest friend and a mind that constantly told me I needed to do better. That's a personality trait that is tough to shake.

I went back to cognitive behavioural therapy and opened up the doors for change. This time, I came armed with my new best friend... my personal formula for wellness: *Fitness and all things health-related.*

With ongoing counselling and moral support again from family and friends, I allowed myself the time and resources to get well again. I pulled back on everything and allowed myself the space to heal physically and psychologically. The groceries were ordered online, I stopped pushing for new business, I allowed others to help me, I walked daily in the sunshine, and ensured I was on the couch relaxing with a chamomile tea by 7 pm. Total self-care.

During this period, I was deep into writing this book, but after discussions with my psychologist, I decided it was best to put it aside. Writing meant I was reliving my darkest days and this was exacerbating my PTSD and pulling me further under. I felt this was another failure, but as the days rolled on, I realised that putting a pause on writing was the right thing to do.

The other breakdown was a few years earlier in 2016 after extensive surgery. The aftermath symptoms were similar but nowhere near as intense as the other episode. I reacted violently to surgery medications—before and after.

As strong as I feel at times, my nervous system still has meltdowns. I live with a mental illness that sometimes feels "invisible" and other times is staring me right in the face.

I am constantly advocating on all of my business and social media platforms that mental health issues need greater educational exposure and compassionate support.

Flashbacks and PTSD are real issues for recovering addicts. It's two-pronged: The reasons why you abused in the first place and what you did when under the influence. There is shame and guilt surging from many angles and a lot of it, once talked through with a professional, can be compartmentalised and put in perspective.

There are so many brilliant quotes that have helped me move through various stages of recovery, many anonymous. One I remind myself of when the demons emerge is: *"You are not what you did in your addiction"*.

The longer I have been sober, the more I recognise that when I was drinking, I was never healing. Drinking prevented me from encouraging my soul to soar. Drinking created a mask I falsely believed would protect me.

Previously, the thought of doing this personal development stuff sober would have been beyond terrifying, but ironically, it was being sober that allowed me to cope.

On my trip to Bali in March 2019 the weight loss was
becoming more evident.

Bali 2019. Despite the challenges that came with that year what I am most proud of is that I didn't pick up a drink.

My Sobriety Step 9

- Recognise early when you are falling off-track.
- Create a checklist of symptoms that occur before a breakdown.
- Ask for help as soon as you need it.
- Be proud of how far you have already come.
- If you relapse analyse why and put a plan in place to get back on track.
- You haven't failed if you are continuing to try.
- Forgive yourself for the past and focus on what magic you can bring to the future.

When you reach the end of your rope, tie a knot in it and hang on.

~ Thomas Jefferson

CHAPTER 10

PRESS REPEAT

O NE of the most pertinent teachings I employed in my recovery process was the importance of routine and, in particular, repeating behaviour.

There's a tendency to associate these with negative and self-sabotaging actions and, in my case, my past was a testament to that. But, as we know, repetition is what allows us to form habits that become automatic... the more we do them, the less resistant we become to them.

My days were prioritised with eating well, training hard, and ensuring I got enough sleep. Clearly, my family came first, but ironically, they were the ones who encouraged this to happen and provided me with every opportunity to progress. They became the advocates for my routine and I will forever be grateful they not only supported my changes but also provided me with the freedom to maintain them. This is what made it all possible.

I have always been a creature of habit, largely due to my OCD tendencies. My childhood was riddled with strange repetitious behaviour and this has remained a major part of my life. Words and phrases constantly ran through my head and I was torn between feeling threatened or trying to take control.

One of my most unsettling times was school holidays. While most students were happily looking forward to the break, I would be fretting about a lack of routine when I went home. It drove me to despair. I can remember being excited on the eve of the new school term. It felt like a relief.

Post-rehab, the benefits of repetitive exercise, associated with a healthy diet, was showing outstanding all-round results.

By 2014, my physical health was in tip-top shape. My liver readings were "exceptional", according to my doctor. My triglycerides were back to normal and all of my extensive blood work showed that my body was not only in complete recovery, it was thriving.

Aesthetically, I looked better than I did in my 20s and I am still amazed at how I was able to shape my 47-year-old body into something beyond my dreams. I am toned, I am lean, and my skin glows with a youthful appearance.

Treating Physician

Dr EPM Fisser

B.Pharm

MBBCh

MRCGP (UK)

FRACGP

POST-DETOX

Justine emerged from detox as a confident, articulate lady with a purpose. Her emotional metamorphosis has been phenomenal. She has endless drive and focus, bounds with energy and with the support of her husband and children, has completely changed her life around. She is an inspiration for anybody overcoming similar obstacles.

Physically, her photos speak for themselves. With a chiselled physique, Justine oozes good health and happiness.

Under the skin, her transformation continues. Her blood test alcohol markers are normal.

As her medical practitioner, I have taken great pleasure in witnessing this wonderful transformation, and I am proud to have been a small part of it. I wish Justine and her family every happiness in the future and look forward to watching her go from strength to strength in the future.

At the peak of my self-medicating, my eyes were sullen, my skin had a yellow/grey tinge, and that alcohol "bloat" was evident even when I looked skeletal.

But the most rewarding part of it all was how I felt psychologically. I was happy.

My panic attacks were minimal and manageable and only brought on by things like lack of sleep and overwhelming myself with too many tasks. The benefits of being "present" had flowed through to my relationships with David and my children. We were tight and we were very connected.

To wake up and not dread what the day had in store for me was something I had not experienced since I was a teenager.

Don't get me wrong, I do not wake up every single day and jump out of bed excited about life. Life on some days still sucks. But I am grateful in the knowledge that whatever the day holds for me, as long as I keep to my routine, I will get through it just fine.

Routine gives me a feeling of being safe. Not having one makes me feel uncomfortable, anxious, and vulnerable. I don't like the unexpected, and that's the OCD talking.

Being okay with not being okay is something I am still working on. I have conceded that if this is the one thing that keeps me sober and prevents me from falling off the wagon, then I really don't mind.

There is a time and place to pick your battles and I think this trait is one I should hang on to.

Part of "pressing repeat" for me is the continued inclination to learn, grow, and develop as a woman, a mother, a wife, and a human being. The minute I think "*I've got this*" is the day it will all turn pear-shaped.

I was given a second, third, and fourth chance to get things right. The goalposts can shift, but the underlying theme will be the same:

- **Stay sober**
- Be well
- **Continue to heal**
- Nurture your mind and body
- **Give back**

- Be present in the moment
- **Forgive yourself**

The foundation of wellness I have created is not foolproof, but it is my most secure way in ensuring all of the above are my focus each and every day in a life where alcohol is not a consideration.

My favourite quote about recovery is "*sobriety delivered everything alcohol promised*". The whole damn lot—the calm, the peace, content, happiness, the joy, the love, the money, forgiveness, body, health, the strength, the power.

And it can for you, too.

My Sobriety Step 10

- Exercise in some shape or form most days.
- Practice self-care regularly.
- Always tell others how you are feeling.
- Continue on the path of self-development.
- Never forget what alcohol took away from you.
- And always remember your 'why'.

Treating Psychologist.

Dr Ian Platt

B Psych (Hons) DPsych (Clin)

Justine has written a personal and moving account of her recovery from alcohol addiction. Our work commenced after her abstinence was well established and I was thus not involved in that remarkable achievement. From a psychological perspective, we have focussed on Justine's anxiety and trauma, and collaborated to try and reach an understanding (as best we can) of factors that may have contributed to anxiety onset in childhood, its subsequent maintenance into adulthood, and issues that were potentially blocking Justine from 'being' in the world as she wished to be.

According to psychological theory, early childhood is a critical period for the development of a sense of self as being worthy, lovable, acceptable, and relatively capable. This comes from a process of 'seeing others see us' (with approval) as we expand our exploration of the world. As a result, we gradually foster a perspective of the world and others as essentially trustworthy and safe.

Through the adolescent years, we progressively look more to our peer group for confirmation that we are acceptable and worthy of love, and most importantly, that we 'belong'.

Many factors (protective and harmful) influence this process and the outcomes in peoples' lives. The interaction of temperament and environment is one such element. This accounts in part for why siblings, who have been exposed to similar circumstances when growing up, can present quite differently in terms of their relative view of self and the world.

If we emerge with doubts as to (for example) the degree others will view us as worthy, acceptable, and competent, we can develop beliefs and behaviours that, we hope, will help us to survive and influence others to meet our needs for love and regard. We may thus become perfectionistic, believing that this is the only way we will find fulfillment and regard. We might anxiously avoid certain situations believing that this will keep us safe.

Whilst these behaviours may be helpful at the time, they can eventually prove maladaptive and dysfunctional later in life. Therapeutic work is not about establishing 'fault' or 'blame' for the difficulties encountered (this is invariably unhelpful). From my clinical perspective it is about helping a person to grow their awareness of unhelpful patterns of beliefs and behaviour, and instigate change that provides a new and improved experience of life. Hopefully, this will provide a basis for a more authentic and less fearful relationship with the world.

When Justine talks about her early life, her anxiety, and how doubts about self were held "with a bit more intensity than the average person", I formed the view that, for whatever reason, Justine had not emerged from childhood with a secure sense of self as worthy and acceptable; she believed that, as a result, others would ultimately reject her. Her ability as a performer allowed her to shine, however her doubts always undermined her achievements. In my experience, this is common nothing ever quite 'did it' in terms of filling the void of worthlessness, no matter how much she strived or the complements she received.

The sense of rejection at the end of her first serious relationship would have been devasting Justine believed that finally she was being seen, accepted, and loved. Heartbreaking for any young person, for Justine the breakup would simply have confirmed her core sense of unworthiness. Humans tend to solve problems by 'making them go away'. For Justine, as she notes, the solution was alcohol. That the alcohol itself caused other problems, including exacerbating her anxiety, was a secondary concern for her.

Justine's description of the ensuing years of alcohol addiction, with episodic attempts at abstinence, is heartbreaking, but not atypical. One particular psychological theory posits that change depends on one's 'readiness' to engage in change. The model, which is not without its critics, proposes that interventions need to be tailored to the state of readiness for change that the individual is 'in'. Thus, for people not remotely wanting to change or considering it, attempting to engage them in, for example, planning for change is unlikely to achieve much. It might, however, be more effective when a person is actively considering changing. During the change process, it is possible that a 'lapse' will occur (as it did in Justine's case), however the lapse does not have to be a return to the beginning. The person has already learned a significant amount about, for example, urge surfing, or drink refusal skills. Learning how to manage a lapse, if it occurs, is thus critical.

Ultimately, and in my clinical experience I have witnessed it regardless of whether the problem is alcohol, other drugs, gambling etc, the key driver of change is the moment that the person says, as Justine did with her drinking, "…this just does not work for me anymore". It is frequently a pivotal moment. From this point, Justine developed a self-care approach which, for her, involved a routinebased health regimen of exercise and diet, in conjunction with compassionate self-talk.

This latter element is particularly important regarding Justine's ongoing recovery from trauma. The experience of trauma puts our adaptive 'alarm system' into a state of ongoing vigilance. Traumatised individuals often feel hostile to the person they were when the trauma occurred – they feel guilty and ruminate on how, in some way, it was their fault or they 'deserved it'. Although the traumatic events are technically a memory, a traumatised mind tends to continue to react as though the events are still happening, or likely to re-occur. Finding kindness and compassion to, in Justine's case, her younger self, in conjunction with the familiarity of routine and spending time with the people who love her and accept her for the person she is have undoubtedly contributed to her feeling safer now.

As a result, Justine is having a new experience of life in a manner that reflects the wise words attributed to Nelson Mandela; "May your choices reflect your hopes, not your fears".

Never be afraid to fall apart because it is an opportunity to rebuild yourself the way you wish you had been all along.

~ Rae Smith

I dedicate this book to these *special people*

MY children, Evelyn and Wilson. You are my reason for recovery and my purpose for living. Every decision I made to get well and stay sober was because I knew you deserved the best version of me. I am still here on Earth because of you. Thank you for the privilege of being your mum.

My husband, David… my best friend, my soul mate, and my lover. The continued love and support you have given me has allowed me to heal and live a life that is full of good health and happiness. Thank you for helping me find my wings.

To my mum, Lesley, and my two dads—Donat (Don) and Chris. If it were not for each of you at different times pulling me out of harm's way and into safety, I would not be here to write this book. You provided me with all of the tools and assistance I needed to recover and stay on track. I am not sure I can ever say 'sorry' enough to compensate for the worry and stress I caused you, but hopefully seeing me today is enough to at least show you that it was worth it.

To my sister, Cassie, you literally saved my life. You sacrificed what you personally needed at the time to keep me afloat. Little sister responsibilities turned into big sister ones. Thank you for everything you have done.

To my brother, Cam. We just get each other. It's unspoken stuff. And I know that you understand me always. Love you, big little bro.

To my late nana, Irene, and grandad, Arthur, you both gave me the gift of writing. Nan, I wrote this book for the two of us to demonstrate that we cannot let fear rule our lives. I miss you so much.

Wayne Ryan Jnr, for passing on your inspiring torch for fitness. This was the game-changer.

My best friend, Louise Edmonds, who not only encouraged me to write my story, but has also been with me every step of the way, championing my every decision and providing me with the right direction and guidance. Lou, you brought me back into heavenly faith and, in turn, my purpose was given an opportunity to soar. Soul sisters forever.

My God Mother Den who helped care for me in Melbourne in the crucial last months before I was able to get to the safe arms of my family in Queensland.

My treating doctors Dr Paul Fisser and Dr Ian Platt for assisting me with both my physical and mental health and generously agreeing to contribute pieces towards this project.

Sandi Louise Ross for continuing to create a natural and holistic approach to my overall health and sharing your wisdom through your words.

All of my friends and support network that have continued to support me in my sober and fitness journey. I love you all from the bottom of my heart.

And finally, for every person who reads this who is trapped in the cycle of alcohol or drug abuse and feels like they are dying from the inside out, I see you, I hear you, and I feel you because I have been you. I promise life on the other side is more beautiful than you can ever imagine.

Printed in Great Britain
by Amazon